Pentecost and Parousia

Pentecost and Parousia

Charismatic Renewal, Christian Unity,
and the Coming Glory

Peter Hocken

With Foreword by
Cecil M. Robeck Jr.

WIPF & STOCK · Eugene, Oregon

PENTECOST AND PAROUSIA
Charismatic Renewal, Christian Unity, and the Coming Glory

Wipf & Stock
An Imprint of Wipf and Stock Publishers
199 8th Ave., Suite 3
Eugene, OR 97401

www.wipfandstock.com

ISBN 13: 978-1-62564-113-7

Manufactured in the U.S.A.

Contents

Foreword

SINCE THE MID-TWENTIETH CENTURY, the charismatic movement has brought new life and vitality to millions of Christians around the world. This is especially true for the Catholic Charismatic Renewal, which claims that as many as 120 million Catholics are part of the renewal. That is one in every ten Catholics in the world! Of course, the renewal is not confined to the Catholic Church, though the Catholic Charismatic Renewal is by far the largest and the best organized of the many charismatic renewal movements within the various families of the church today. Still, as with all denominations, the number and percentage of Catholics who participate in the Catholic Charismatic Renewal varies from country to country, and its success has been partially dependent upon the support of the bishops in those countries, some of whom have been more supportive than others. The same may be said of the success or failure of the charismatic movement in all Christian families or denominations. But charismatic renewal is not about bishops and other Christian leaders, nor is it ultimately about the numbers of participants it has attracted. It is about God; especially the Third Person of the Trinity, the Holy Spirit, and it is about the openness of God's people to allow the Holy Spirit to accomplish the work of God in and through their lives.

All four Gospel writers introduce us to the ministry of Jesus by telling us that baptism in or with the Holy Spirit will be linked directly to the ministry of Jesus. John the Baptist informed his followers that Jesus would bring a baptism of Spirit and fire (Matt 3:11; Mark 1:8; Luke 3:16; John 1:33). And when John baptized Jesus, he bore witness to the fact that the Spirit descended upon Jesus in the form of a dove (Matt 3:16; Mark 1:10; Luke 3:22; John 1:32).

Throughout his ministry, Jesus often spoke of the Holy Spirit. It is John's gospel that records some of the clearest points that Jesus made regarding the Spirit. He knew that before very long, he would be leaving his disciples. He told them that when he returned to the Father, he would ask the Father to send the Paraclete to be with them (John 14:16). The Spirit would work throughout the world, both within and outside of the church. While the outside world is unaware of the Spirit's presence because they cannot receive him (John 13:15), the Holy Spirit is nonetheless active in the world, convincing the world of sin, of righteousness, and of judgment (John 16:8–11). The Spirit's primary role within the church is to bear witness to and glorify Jesus (John 15:26; 16:14). The Holy Spirit does not come on his own authority (John 16:13), but teaches us and reminds us of what Jesus has taught (John 14:26), taking that which Jesus wants us to know and declaring it to us (John 16:14).

When we add all of these things together, we can see that the coming of the Spirit is extremely important to the birth and to the ongoing life and health of the church. The Holy Spirit brings life and vitality. The Holy Spirit has been sent to make a difference in our lives. The Spirit unifies us. The Spirit sets us apart and makes us holy. The Apostle Paul tells us that the Spirit has given each of us gifts that are intended to contribute something to the welfare of the body of Christ. These charismatic endowments are given solely in keeping with the sovereign will of the Holy Spirit (1 Cor 12:11), and the goal is that we will use them in loving ways (1 Cor 13:1–13) to build up the body of Christ (1 Cor 14:1–12) and to bring glory to God (1 Cor 14:22–25). To forget these things, not to act upon these things, is to forget who we are and who we are intended to be. The charismatic movement is a reminder that we are the body of Christ, set apart from the world, indwelt by the Holy Spirit of God who has made us one so that we might become witnesses to the world around us of the reconciling power of God. This is the reason that Jesus instructed his followers to go to Jerusalem and wait for the promise of the Father.

Since at least the time of the Cappadocians in the fourth century, the church has held that the Holy Spirit is God, and as such, the Holy Spirit is worthy of our worship. And for centuries, the church has invoked the Spirit in its services of worship. It has often prayed, "Come, Holy Spirit." But once the Holy Spirit was invoked, it seemed to be the case that there was nothing further for the Spirit to do, nothing further on which to act. Compare that reality with the observation of the New Testament scholar B. H. Streeter, who noted some seventy-five years ago that the earliest Christians seem to have experienced the Holy Spirit in ways "as definite and observable as . . . an attack of influenza."[1] How do we account for this taming of the Holy Spirit?

Whatever the response we might make to this question, a number of events during the twentieth century changed all that. These events included but were not limited to the Apostolic Exhortation and the encyclical penned by Pope Leo XIII that recommended to Catholics a nine-day novena of prayer for the Holy Spirit as the world entered the twentieth century. As the New Year broke in 1901, Pope Leo XIII prayed the hymn of the Holy Spirit, thereby giving the Spirit greater visibility in the church. The early twentieth century also saw the birth of the modern Pentecostal movement, which has for more than a century borne witness to the person and work of the Holy Spirit throughout the world. In 1959, charismatic renewal became public within Episcopalian and soon after within Protestant congregations in the United States. With the prayer of Pope John XXIII for a "New Pentecost" in 1961, the Second Vatican Council (1962–1965) was ushered in. During that council the Holy Spirit and the charisms were studied and the bishops took great care to encourage broader recognition of both the person and the work of the Holy Spirit in the church. Very shortly after the council (1967), the charismatic renewal appeared in the Catholic Church. The Catholic charismatic renewal has been well received and encouraged by every pope since and it has contributed substantially to the health and vitality of the Catholic Church around the world. Yet the widespread presence of the charismatic movement in Catholic, Orthodox, Anglican, and Protestant churches, to say nothing of the Pentecostal movement demonstrates quite clearly that the renewal is intrinsically ecumenical in its promise.

Fr. Peter Hocken is exactly the right person to tell the story of the birth and expansion of this vital movement. He has been a participant in the Catholic charismatic renewal since 1971, as well as a participant-observer in the broader charismatic renewal that has swept through many denominations. He has also been an able theologian to the larger charismatic renewal and working among Pentecostals of all stripes, providing them with wise counsel and informed criticism for over four decades. His participation in the Renewal in the United States as well as a number of European countries, has given him a bird's eye view of how the charismatic renewal functions in various locations. In this book he sets forth the story of the renewal and

---

1. Streeter, *Primitive Church*, 69.

then he draws on several major theological themes to explain its presence, its challenges, and its contributions.

As we have moved into the twenty-first century, we have been made aware of a significant number of changes in religious life around the world. While Christianity may finally be viewed as a truly global religion with Christian voices in most every country around the world, they are sometimes at odds with one another. In spite of the large body of doctrine and practice that they share, there is still considerable disunity between many of them. There is a tendency to emphasize their differences rather than those things that they hold in common. Yet with a total membership of approximately 2.3 billion people, the church still finds itself living with a minority status in a world that boasts a population of over seven billion souls, and in many places the church is a highly persecuted minority.

At the present time, nearly 300 million people are constantly on the move, the result of a variety of factors—war, genocide and/or ethnic cleansing, famine, economic promise, the expulsion of minorities or forced relocations, and either the violation of or the hope for expanded human rights. While many of these people are members of other religions, a surprising number of them are Christians, and many of them are part of the charismatic movement in one form or another. The teaching and experiences they have gleaned through their participation in the charismatic movement have provided them with peace, purpose, and power as they seek to live out their Christian lives in new, foreign, and sometimes hostile contexts.

In addition, with the increased pressures of secularism, the new atheism, the breakdown of traditional values surrounding family, life, and sexuality, the lack of trust by young people as they think about traditional institutions and the power that they have held in the past, as well as new emphases on spirituality rather than religiosity, the church is situated in the middle of massive change. One may wonder what role, if any, the now substantial Pentecostal movement and the very significant charismatic movement might play together in addressing these and related concerns.

As an astute observer of the world around him and as a fine theologian who has studied both Scripture and the charismatic renewal, Fr. Hocken has much to contribute to our understanding of and appreciation for this vital movement. In this volume, Fr. Hocken explores the ecumenical contribution of the charismatic renewal, especially as it is lived out by faithful Catholics, though he has clearly reached out to many other facets of the charismatic movement. At one level, this is a study in ecclesiology, the doctrine of the church, intended to help the church to embrace the presence and power of the Holy Spirit with new intentionality. At other levels, it provides challenges to how we live as Christians, both individually and in community, to what we should see as values to be supported, and how we might draw upon the renewing power of the Holy Spirit to accomplish the important work that the Lord intends to accomplish in and through us.

Many books have been written about the charismatic movement over the past half century, but only at this point is it possible to track where the movement has been in such a way as to be able to posit a trajectory of where it might go next. Fr. Hocken not only reminds us that the charismatic movement is rooted in the church of this world and bringing power for our daily lives, but with its arms stretched heavenward, he demonstrates that the charismatic movement also provides a window on things to come. It plays a prophetic role within the church that draws us forward day by day toward the glorious eschaton when Jesus Christ will return for his own. The life-giving Holy Spirit makes real the hope that is within us. Not only has the Holy Spirit made us one by baptizing us into Jesus Christ, but the Holy Spirit continues to draw us into a oneness that can only be had through the work of the Holy Spirit in our lives.

Cecil M. Robeck Jr.
Professor of Church History and Ecumenics
Director of the David J. du Plessis Center for Christian Spirituality
Fuller Theological Seminary
135 North Oakland Ave.
Pasadena, California 91182, USA

Introduction

My involvement in the charismatic movement dates back to 1971. I was praying in Edgbaston, Birmingham, England, with a small group of Catholics who had already entered into this dimension of Christian experience. The others were singing in the Spirit, and I immediately knew that I could join in. So I began singing in tongues without any imposition of hands, or prayer for the baptism in the Spirit. This act of faith opened a new chapter in my life. The following Saturday these friends took me to a remarkable Pentecostal church in Hockley, a rundown inner city suburb of Birmingham. That evening was an eye-opener for me, a Catholic priest teaching moral theology in the diocesan seminary.

At that time the only entrance into this church led through a tunnel. As we advanced down the tunnel, the noise of music and joy-filled praise grew louder. I had an impression of the early Christians entering the catacombs. As the revival evening progressed, this sense of encountering the power and dynamism of primitive Christian faith remained with me. Hockley Pentecostal Church was pastored by two women, always known as Miss Reeve and Miss Fisher, both in their seventies, both who had been there for over thirty years. They were very different personalities. Miss Reeve, less demonstrative, a peaceful presence on the platform; she gave rich prophecies couched in King James English and full of biblical allusions. Miss Fisher was more vigorous, exuding spiritual strength as she danced, and as she ministered; her laying on hands was no delicate gesture. But what impressed me most was their total openness to the Holy Spirit and their sense of spiritual authority. Those were early days in the Catholic charismatic renewal, and not all Pentecostals were convinced of its authenticity. But these two women were always welcoming, even calling me "dear brother father." Once when a visiting preacher made some anti-Catholic remarks, they later called a sister to the platform to share the wonderful things God was doing among the Roman Catholics.

The Hockley experience had a major impact on my ministry. First, it gave me a great love for the Pentecostals. Even though I later visited Pentecostal services that were not as dynamic as Hockley, and I met Pentecostals who were not so evidently filled with the Spirit as Miss Reeve and Miss Fisher, I knew deep down that the Pentecostal movement was from God, and was of huge importance for the whole world and the whole church. Second, I never for a moment thought of becoming a Pentecostal. I was a committed Catholic convert, deeply impacted by the whole church experience of the Second Vatican Council. So I instinctively understood that the charismatic renewal as it came to be known was the entrance of this Pentecostal grace and fire into the other Christian churches. It was not Pentecostal theology or Pentecostal doctrine that impressed me, but the faith life of Pentecostals—their simplicity, their love of the Lord, and their confidence in the power of the Holy Spirit made manifest in signs and wonders.

As a Catholic excited by Vatican Two and already deeply involved in ecumenical relations, I immediately sensed the importance for Christian unity of this spread of Pentecostal grace to the rest of the Christian world. I knew that the instinct of many charismatic Christians to distance themselves from the Pentecostals was not from the Lord. For many, it seemed as though the main lesson to learn from the Pentecostals was to avoid their excesses. But I also became aware of the parallel trend on the Pentecostal side, of being very cautious in relation to the charismatics, as though they posed a danger to the purity of Pentecostal faith. As I entered more deeply into the charismatic renewal, I knew that I had to contend for the ecumenical character of this outpouring of the Holy Spirit. I also sensed that this would not be easy, as insistence on this ecumenical grace would come up against the deep suspicions of Christians on all sides.

Third, I received a desire to learn more about the Pentecostals, especially their origins. A few years later when I had the opportunity to study for a PhD, I was able to research the Pentecostal origins in the USA, in Canada, in Great Britain, and in France, perusing the remarkable periodicals and bulletins that were produced in the first years. I came to love and admire their great heroes of faith: Willie Burton, Lillian Trasher, Smith Wigglesworth, Douglas Scott, Alice Belle Garrigus. From all these experiences and convictions came my involvement in Pentecostal studies and the development of many friendships with Pentecostal leaders and scholars. I should acknowledge that I received as warm a welcome, though in a different register, at the Society for Pentecostal Studies as I had earlier at Hockley Pentecostal Church.

This is my second book on the charismatic movement and Christian unity. The first, *One Lord One Spirit One Body*, was written to be available at the 1987 interdenominational charismatic conference in New Orleans. My hope was to communicate this broader vision of the power of the Holy Spirit for reconciliation and unity in a way accessible to all in the renewal movement. It was aimed at ordinary participants, and sought to be as simple as possible. Maybe at that time I had not gauged the degree of resistance to accepting baptism in the Spirit and the spiritual gifts as a major stimulus from the Lord for Christian reconciliation. In this new book I look at the evidence for this ecumenical grace and at the history of its reception; I suggest that the present time is more propitious for a second reception, and for an interaction of this outpouring of the Holy Spirit with the ecumenical movement for Christian unity. Finally, I look at some of the theological issues that have arisen, how they can contribute to a new dynamism for Christian reconciliation, and to the full coming of the kingdom of God.

To argue for a coming together of the ancient Christian churches deeply attached to their traditions with the whole chaotic world of Pentecostal and charismatic effervescence may seem totally utopian and unrealistic. It is a visionary dream. Humanly speaking, it is impossible. But it is a sign of the outpouring of the Spirit that "your young men shall see visions and your old men shall dream dreams" (Acts 2:17 citing Joel 2:28). Already we have seen improbable if not impossible things taking place: Catholics speaking in tongues; the same course of evangelism being used by Christians across the whole spectrum from Catholics to Pentecostals and new church charismatics; the pope calling for Catholics to repent of the sins of the past; a future pope kneeling to receive blessing from Pentecostal leaders in Latin America; Jews believing in Jesus and insisting they are still Jews. I see that I received this vision at Hockley. There is much evidence that this vision and these dreams are from the Holy Spirit. Out of touch with reality? In touch with the Holy Spirit? That is for each reader to determine.

Peter Hocken
Hainburg an der Donau, Austria
May 2013

Abbreviations

CCC	*Catechism of the Catholic Church*. New York: Doubleday, 1994.
CCR	Catholic Charismatic Renewal
CCL	*Code of Canon Law*. London: Collins, 1983.
CRECES	Comunión Renovada de Evangélicos y Católicos en el Espíritu Santo (Renewed Communion of Catholics and Evangelicals in the Holy Spirit)
DV	*Dei Verbum* (Constitution on Divine Revelation of the Second Vatican Council)
ECCLA	Encuentro Catolico Carismatico Latinoamericano
GCF	Global Christian Forum
HJ	*The Heythrop Journal*. Heythrop College, University of London, England.
ICCOWE	International Charismatic Consultation on World Evangelization
ICCRS	International Catholic Charismatic Renewal Services
LG	*Lumen Gentium* (Constitution on the Church of the Second Vatican Council)
NA	*Nostra Aetate* (Declaration on Non-Christian Religions of the Second Vatican Council)
NC	*New Covenant Magazine*

NIDPCM	*The New International Dictionary of Pentecostal and Charismatic Movements.* Edited by Stanley M. Burgess and Eduard M. van der Maas. Grand Rapids, MI: Zondervan, 2002.
PO	*Presbyterorum Ordinis* (Decree on the Ministry and Life of Priests of the Second Vatican Council)
RH	*Redemptor Hominis.* London: Catholic Truth Society, 1979. (Encyclical Letter of John Paul II)
RM	*Redemptoris Mater.* London: Catholic Truth Society, 1987. (Encyclical Letter of John Paul II)
SC	*Sacrosanctum Concilium* (Constitution on the Liturgy of the Second Vatican Council)
SPS	Society for Pentecostal Studies
TJCII	Toward Jerusalem Council II
TMA	*Tertio Millennio Adveniente* (Apostolic Letter of John Paul II). Vatican City: Libreria Editrice Vaticana, 1994.
UR	*Unitatis Redintegratio* (Decree on Ecumenism of the Second Vatican Council)
UUS	*Ut Unum Sint.* English translation. London: Catholic Truth Society, 1995. (Encyclical Letter of John Paul II)
WCC	World Council of Churches

I

Charismatic Renewal
is Inherently Ecumenical

1

A Major Surprise of the Holy Spirit

AFTER THE DISCIPLES HAD witnessed many healings and works of power during the ministry of Jesus, and when the seventy "returned with joy" from their mission (Luke 10:17), Jesus told them: "Blessed are the eyes which see what you see! For I tell you that many prophets and kings desired to see what you see, and did not see it, and to hear what you hear, and did not hear it" (Luke 10:23–24). I have often been reminded of these words during forty years of experience in the charismatic renewal, particularly when I was witnessing things that I never imagined I would ever see. Prominent among these eye-opening moments have been experiences of deep fellowship and reconciliation across ecclesial and denominational divides. In this book on the ecumenical character and potential of the charismatic movement, I want to highlight the role of the Holy Spirit in the breaking down of barriers, and in the establishment of deep respectful relationships between Christians from very different traditions and backgrounds.

From 1977, I can recall the banner-filled arena at Atlantic City, New Jersey, where twenty-five thousand Catholics had been raising their arms and moving their bodies in full-blooded joyful praise of the Lord. This Catholic crowd was drinking in with appreciation the Bible teaching of Robert Frost, a nondenominational pastor. The whole scene presented a vision of a different church—not replacing the Catholic Church, but simply a church being brought to life by the Holy Spirit. I recall too a moment from the European Charismatic Leaders conference in Paris in 1982, when a British Pentecostal pastor repented for his wrong attitudes to Catholics, and for walking out in protest from the first Fountain Trust meeting in England at which there was a Catholic speaker.[1] From Brighton, England, in 1991, I can remember a stirring message from Fr. Raniero Cantalamessa, OFM Cap, the preacher to the papal household, that brought the mixed crowd of Anglicans, Baptists, Pentecostals, Catholics, and many others to a moment of profound silence and common penitence before the living God. From Buenos Aires, Argentina, in 2005, I cannot forget the moment when following my Catholic confession of the evils of the Spanish and Portuguese Inquisitions, a lady Baptist pastor addressed me as brother, hugged me, and said, "I have never called a Catholic priest brother before." Another such moment was in 2011, when a prophetic team prayed for me at the International House of Prayer in Kansas City. How astonished I was when this team of four young people, none of them Catholics, who knew nothing about my identity or my life, proceeded to touch on virtually all the significant areas in my service of the Lord.

Such moments of astonishment at the visible working of the Holy Spirit across the churches and confessions can shake a non-believing or half-believing church out of her complacency. I believe that an objective reflection on the Pentecostal and charismatic movements of the last hundred years will reveal, despite the evident follies and weaknesses, an extraordinary current of new life and power that is changing the face of world Christianity.[2]

The Charismatic Movement

The charismatic movement of the Spirit is itself a major surprise. It offends secularizing theologies by its unashamedly interventionist character. It is an irruption, an outbreak, in our midst of the love and power of the risen Lord Jesus Christ. No church or denomination was looking for or expecting this kind of renewal. Among the historic churches, overt enthusiasm was hardly the order of the day. Testifying to the impact of Jesus on one's life was frowned on as an expression of Evangelical naiveté.

Speaking in other tongues was the most striking symbol of this irruption of the unfamiliar into Christian life. By its nature, the making of

1. The Pentecostal was Alfred Missen, who had been general secretary of the Assemblies of God in Britain and Ireland. See Au, *Grassroots Unity*, 121. The Fountain Trust conference was at Guildford in July 1971, and Kevin Ranaghan was the Catholic speaker.

2. Philip Jenkins presents this basic thesis in his book *The Next Christendom*.

unintelligible sounds by adults is offensive to the intelligence. For the mainline Protestant churches, more infected by a rationalist spirit, this irrational feature of the charismatic movement caused the most discomfort. The Catholic Church, more familiar with extravagant piety and claims to the supernatural, was not so worried by glossolalia, but still found it difficult to see anything significant in such phenomena. How could making unintelligible sounds contribute anything serious to the renewal of Christian faith?

I see three main elements in this surprise of the Holy Spirit. The first is simply the depth and scope of what was happening in the charismatic movement. God was visiting Christians of all shades and stripes. They were receiving a deep love for the Lord Jesus in their hearts, hearing his voice, and experiencing his power to deliver from evil. They could praise the Lord spontaneously in their own words and in their own prayer-language. The Scriptures came alive, disclosing the face of the one Savior and Lord. There reappeared in the church the spiritual gifts listed in 1 Corinthians 12:8–10, that were widely regarded as a curiosity of the apostolic age. Many recipients were clearly neither holy nor mature, which upset the assumption that such gifts were rarely bestowed, and only then as a reward for years of ascetical struggle and purification.

Second, there was the speed with which the charismatic renewal in the Catholic Church was spreading, first in the United States and then around the world. The love of Jesus and the power of the Spirit are infectious. In the United States, attendance at the annual conferences at Notre Dame jumped from thirteen hundred in 1970, to almost five thousand in 1971, to over eleven thousand in 1972, to more than twenty thousand in 1973, and thirty thousand in 1976. Within a few years, the Catholic Charismatic Renewal (CCR) could be found on all continents and in more and more countries.

Third, there was the speed with which the CCR was welcomed at the highest levels of the Catholic Church. The church that seemed the least likely to accept this move of the Spirit welcomed it faster and more explicitly than any other. In just eight years, this movement went from a retreat weekend for students with twenty-five to thirty laypeople near Pittsburgh, Pennsylvania, to a worldwide celebration of twenty thousand in Rome in 1975, at which Pope Paul VI declared that the Renewal was "a chance for the church!" A key factor in this church acceptance was the participation and support of the primate of Belgium, Cardinal Léon Joseph Suenens, one of the great figures of the Second Vatican Council much trusted by the pope.

Its Ecumenical Character

No less amazing than the content of the charismatic "grace" and the rapidity of its spread throughout the world was its appearance across virtually the whole Christian spectrum. The charismatic renewal is the first movement of spiritual revival to impact significantly both the Protestant and the Catholic worlds. For the first time since the Protestant Reformation a current of the Holy Spirit has not only impacted the divided churches, but has brought Catholics and Protestants together in worship, teaching, and prayer ministry. This is a remarkable development that has not been sufficiently appreciated. From its beginnings in the 1960s, Catholics have entered into this blessing through Protestants, and Protestants have entered through Catholics. It cannot be that the interdenominational character of the charismatic movement has little or no significance for the work of Christian unity and reconciliation. Moreover, the official welcome given to CCR by the Catholic authorities represents the first time that a movement that began outside the Catholic communion has been so received. However, the welcome was an acceptance of the movement among Catholics, not official recognition of its interchurch character or ecumenical significance.

The ecumenical character of the renewal is demonstrated above all by the evident fact that the Lord is pouring out the same gifts and graces across the Christian world. The fundamental hallmarks of the renewal are the same everywhere, even though there are differences of style, emphasis, and theological explanation. The witnesses to baptism in the Spirit testify to the same work of the risen Lord: the Spirit's revelation of the crucified and glorious Lord Jesus, the Spirit's opening up of the Scriptures, a hearing of the Lord's voice, the release of spontaneous praise and adoration, the desire and the ability to evangelize, the reception of the spiritual gifts or charisms, a new awareness of the powers of darkness and of the power of the Lord to expose and expel them, and a love for the poor, the needy, and the lost. Not only are these characteristics found across church frontiers, but these gifts and endowments can be exercised together, for example in common praise or joint evangelization.

The Ecumenical Origins

I use the term "ecumenical" deliberately in relation to the origins of CCR. This term normally connotes a commitment to Christian unity and the healing of ancient divisions. Was the charismatic movement across the churches and confessions an ecumenical phenomenon in this sense? Probably not. The movement was certainly interdenominational, but it did not have Christian unity as a goal. Many charismatic Christians in the Protestant churches did sense the importance of the charismatic movement for Christian unity. But quite a number shared the common Pentecostal view that ecumenism is a manmade effort to bring together largely dead and ineffective churches. Only with the beginning of CCR did a fully ecumenical vision of this phenomenon become possible. For the Second Vatican Council had recently committed the Catholic Church to an ecumenical vision, and the first Catholics in the Renewal all understood this sharing in the Spirit with other Christians in this ecumenical context.

Because the vision of renewal in CCR was for ecclesial renewal, it could not be understood simply in personal terms, but had to embrace the renewal of the church in all its aspects, including the institutional. For this reason the beginning of CCR made possible and necessary a fully ecumenical vision of this whole move of the Spirit. Thus it is important to understand the interdenominational origins of CCR, and to interpret this fact as an ecumenical grace. A study of the way that CCR began in many different countries shows that the Lord frequently used Protestant and Pentecostal instruments to bring this charismatic experience and grace into the Catholic Church.[3] We begin, appropriately, with the event in the USA that in effect launched the renewal as a dynamic movement within the worldwide Catholic Church.

USA

As a movement, CCR was birthed during the weekend of February 18, 1967, at a retreat house called the Ark and the Dove, north of Pittsburgh, Pennsylvania. Some accounts simply mention that this weekend gathered about twenty-five students from Duquesne University, itself dedicated to the Holy Spirit, along with one priest, two faculty members, and one of their wives, all Catholics. After the initial account of Kevin and Dorothy Ranaghan in their book *Catholic Pentecostals*, we now have a fuller account in which one of the participants at the weekend, Patti Gallagher, now Patti Gallagher Mansfield, has tracked down the pre-history. She demonstrates clearly how

3. See chapter 8 for the ecumenical contribution of the charismatic renewal to Christian and ecclesial reconciliation, both actual and potential.

this move of the Spirit had been prepared through a range of contacts with charismatic Protestants.[4] Of particular importance in the background were the circles of Catholic friends with shared activities linking students from Duquesne, Pittsburgh, and the University of Notre Dame, Indiana, with a zeal for the renewal vision of the Second Vatican Council. Of particular importance was the ministry of two young laymen, Ralph Martin and Steve Clark, who worked for the Cursillo movement between 1965 and 1970. Among these circles, two books testifying to the renewing power of baptism in the Spirit were to play a key role: *The Cross and the Switchblade* by David Wilkerson, at that time a Pentecostal preacher, and *They Speak with Other Tongues*, an account by John Sherrill of the charismatic movement in the Protestant churches during the previous ten to fifteen years. Several Catholics who read these books began to think and pray seriously about baptism in the Holy Spirit. Among them were two faculty members from Duquesne, Ralph Keifer and Patrick Bourgeois, who read these books upon the recommendations of Martin and Clark at the National Cursillo Convention in August 1966. These men were spiritually thirsty for "the baptism," and they puzzled over how to proceed. Finally, they decided they should make contact with charismatic Protestants, who had remained in their denomination after being baptized in the Spirit. An Episcopal priest introduced them to a lady parishioner, Betty Shoemaker, who invited them to a prayer meeting at the home of Florence Dodge, a charismatic Presbyterian. Four men from Duquesne attended this prayer meeting on January 13, 1967, and two returned the following Friday. Here the Holy Spirit was preparing for the Duquesne weekend, and here two of the faculty members were baptized in the Spirit.

Accounts of the Duquesne weekend show that there was no public ministry for the students to be baptized in the Spirit. Faculty members did not share their experience, but they gave input, along with Betty Shoemaker. The outpouring of the Holy Spirit happened in an unusual way. Students making impromptu visits to the chapel found themselves transfixed by the majesty of the Lord Jesus. More and more were drawn there and just stayed. Patti Mansfield recalls, "Some people were weeping. Later they said that they felt God's love for them so intensely, they couldn't do anything but weep. Others began to giggle and laugh for sheer joy. Some people, like myself, felt a tremendous burning going through their hands or arms like

---

4. Mansfield, *New Pentecost*.

fire. Others felt a clicking in their throats or a tingling in their tongues."[5] As this outbreak spread to the University of Notre Dame in Indiana within the next two weeks, Ray Bullard, a Pentecostal belonging to the Full Gospel Business Men, was a support to these young Catholics.[6]

As these events generated publicity and the renewal movement spread, word surfaced that in fact some Catholics had already been baptized in the Spirit in other places through non-Catholic sources. A few Catholics, including Barbara Shlemon, had received baptism of the Spirit in 1965 in the Episcopalian parish of Dennis Bennett in Seattle, while the Dominican Francis MacNutt had received it in Tennessee through the influence of the Episcopalian healer Agnes Sanford. These people immediately identified with CCR as it spread out from Pittsburgh, from Notre Dame, and from Ann Arbor, Michigan.

United Kingdom

In England there were two separate strands in the origins of CCR. One was the movement arriving from the USA, the other was indigenous. Some young Dominicans from Blackfriars, Oxford, were deeply impacted through association with Pentecostals from the Elim Pentecostal Church in Oxford. Every Friday evening a prayer meeting was held in Denton, a village near Oxford, in the home of Pentecostal Joan Steele. Out of his experience in Denton came Simon Tugwell's book *Did You Receive the Spirit?* Word spread quickly among some Catholics, and people started traveling weekly to Denton, returning in the early hours of Saturday morning. Myles Dempsey was one of these, and later founded the New Dawn conferences now spreading from England to other lands. Among those much influenced by Fr. Tugwell and the Denton prayer meetings were some Catholics from Birmingham, who were greatly blessed at a remarkable Pentecostal church in Hockley, Birmingham. I myself came into the renewal through the Tugwell stream, which meant that my initial charismatic learning was as much from Hockley Pentecostal Church as it was from CCR sources for which this dimension was still very new.[7] I was teaching moral theology in the Birmingham seminary at that time, and my evaluation of Pentecostal

---

5. Mansfield, *New Pentecost*, 45.

6. Ibid., 9–31; and Ranaghan and Ranaghan, *Catholic Pentecostals*, 6–23.

7. See the Introduction. Hocken, "Significance," owes much to the Hockley experience.

practices and attitudes was influenced by Tugwell's interest in the early Dominicans, and by my own study of Catholic spirituality.[8]

Ireland

In the republic of Ireland, CCR began with some religious sisters who had heard about sisters elsewhere being baptized in the Spirit, and with a meeting between Fr. Joe McGeady and a Presbyterian student, Alan Mitchell. They organized a meeting in Dublin in October 1971, at which the speakers were Fr. McGeady and a Presbyterian pastor, Tom Smail.[9] In early 1972, regular prayer meetings began, and soon a charismatic Quaker, Charles Lamb, began to attend.[10] An Anglican priest from Belfast, Cecil Kerr, met some Catholics in Dublin and invited them to the north, which led to his association with two Belfast Catholics, Larry Kelly and Frank Forte. At the first National Irish Conference in Dublin in 1974, Catholics and Protestants came together, and Ireland became the only country where the National Service Committee (NSC) had some Protestant members. This lasted for two or three years until the Protestants were asked to leave for fear that their involvement might jeopardize church approval of the Renewal. But in the north a service committee was formed with Catholic, Anglican, Methodist, and Baptist members. For many years, this group hosted an annual conference with both Catholic and Protestant speakers, the only public gathering of Christians from both sides in the divided state of Northern Ireland, a witness that provoked annual protests from followers of the Rev. Ian Paisley.

France

Charismatic renewal first entered the Catholic Church in France through French visitors to the USA, the le Pichons from Brest, and Fr. (later Bishop) Albert de Monléon, OP. From the first Catholic contacts came the formation of the Emmanuel community in Paris. But a visit of Père Jean-Paul Régimbal from Granby, Québec, from November through December 1971 gave

8. During this time, Archbishop George Patrick Dwyer of Birmingham asked the author to prepare a report on the Catholic renewal, then still called Catholic Pentecostalism, for the theology commission of the Bishops' Conference of England and Wales. See Hocken, "Catholic."

9. Smail later became an Anglican.

10. For the Irish origins see Flynn, *Charismatic Renewal*; and Lamb, *New Path*.

charismatic renewal an important boost. Fr. Régimbal had been invited to France by two Pentecostal pastors from a center in Carhaix, Brittany, where he began his teaching. He prayed for a priest in Le Mans, together with Pastor Clément le Cossec, and spent an afternoon with Fr. de Monléon, OP. A little later, two American Episcopalians arrived in Lyon from Taizé, asking for the charismatic prayer group, and making contact with Mike, an American Jesuit student already in the renewal. There followed a weekend at a mountain chalet near Grenoble, with the two American visitors, plus Mike and two Jesuit students, Laurent Fabre and Bertrand Lepesant, both future founders of renewal communities. During the weekend, Fabre and Lepesant asked the visitors to lay hands on them, and they were baptized in the Spirit.[11] A German Jesuit, subsequently a leader in CCR in West Germany, Fr. Hubertus Tommek, also received in Lyon at Pentecost 1972.[12] Many French Catholics entered the charismatic experience at the annual charismatic interdenominational conventions organized by the remarkable Pentecostal pioneer Thomas Roberts at la Porte Ouverte near Chalon-sur-Saône, where Roberts had hosted the first inter-confessional charismatic convention in 1971 with David du Plessis and several theologians.[13]

Belgium

A Flemish priest, Fr. Jan Biesbrouck, who later played a leading role in the renewal in Flanders, had been baptized in the Spirit in 1965 during a visit of David du Plessis to Utrecht in the Netherlands.

Colombia

The heart of CCR in Colombia since the beginning has been the community of El Minuto de Dios in Bogota, built up since the 1950s by Fr. Rafael Garcia-Herreros. Fr. Garcia-Herreros had in fact been baptized in the Spirit through the ministry visit of Protestant pastor Harald Bredesen from the USA in around 1968, but he did not want to publicize this experience until he could see how it could be received into a Catholic context. So when Fr.

---

11. See Fabre, *Renouveau*.

12. When the term "received" is mentioned in the context of the spread of the charismatic renewal, it means that the person or persons were baptized in the Spirit.

13. These included J. Rodman Williams (Presbyterian, USA); Fr. Albert de Monléon, OP (France); and Fr. Kilian McDonnell, OSB (USA).

Francis MacNutt, OP visited Bogota in February 1972, Fr. Garcia-Herreros heard about the worldwide CCR and seized the opportunity to plan a Latin American conference, which was held in February 1973.[14] From this point El Minuto de Dios became the center of diffusion of CCR in Colombia.[15] Out of this conference grew ECCLA (Encuentro Catolico Carismatico Latinoamericano), a body that organizes regular meetings of the leaders of CCR in Latin America.

Argentina

In September 1968, Fr. Alberto Ibáñez Padilla, SJ from Buenos Aires was present at the Latin American Bishops' conference (CELAM) in Medellin, Colombia. In the next two months he took part in a pastoral liturgy course in Medellin, and as part of this course visited a number of Protestant and Pentecostal services each week. His conclusion was that Protestant worship was less alive and less participatory than the Catholic, except for the Pentecostals. He was amazed by Pentecostal worship with its freedom within structure and its high level of participation. Then in December 1968, Fr. Ibáñez was impressed by a charismatic prayer meeting during a visit to Fordham University in the USA. On his way home he visited Santiago, Chile, where he shared his Fordham experience, and, subsequently, a prayer group started. Returning to Argentina in April 1969, Fr. Ibáñez wrote an article entitled, "Catholic Pentecostals." A Pentecostal read this article and invited Fr. Ibáñez to visit the church of Pastor Juan Carlos Ortiz.[16] He began attending this church anonymously each week and saw how it was growing steadily in numbers. After two months, he revealed his identity, and they offered to pray over him for baptism in the Spirit. He experienced nothing at that moment, but four days later, meditating in his bedroom, Fr. Ibáñez experienced a great flow of tongues coming out of his mouth. Soon after, some people from the Free Brethren came to Juan Carlos Ortiz wanting to know about this move of the Spirit. As a result a group of twelve leaders

14. From Doll, "Colombia," 20–21. This report does not mention the name of the Protestant pastor, but I was given his name in a personal meeting with Harald Bredesen in Escondido, California, many years later.

15. What began as a social ministry grew into a community, which in turn rendered many services. See Jaramillo, "It Can be Done," 2.

16. In the 1970s, Juan Carlos Ortiz was the best known internationally of the Argentinian Pentecostals, due to his teaching on discipleship.

from various churches met regularly for a time with Ortiz, Orville Swindoll (Free Brethren), nine leading Evangelicals, and Fr. Ibáñez.[17]

Some Other Nations in Latin America

An important stimulus at the start of CCR in several Latin American nations was a number of visits by an ecumenical team from the USA working with local Catholic Sisters and Protestant pastors. These trips were the inspiration of a Methodist pastor who wanted Catholics to join them for Latin American outreach. Core members of this team visiting Costa Rica, Peru, and Bolivia were Fr. Francis MacNutt, OP and two Methodist ministers, Rev. Tommy Tyson and Rev. Joe Petree. Soon after, ecumenical teams visited Ecuador and Chile.[18]

Ghana

People from three charismatic streams came together to form the Catholic charismatic renewal in Ghana. First, a group of ten young Catholics gathered around Anthony Osei-Assibey, later national coordinator with CCR, who had been fellowshiping with the Bible Study and Prayer Group of the Presbyterian Church of Ghana.[19] Second, there was a Holy Spirit sister exposed to CCR during a stay in the USA. Third, a prayer group started at the University of Ghana in Legon had interchurch connections.[20]

South Korea

CCR in Korea owes its origins to a Swedish Pentecostal woman, Ms. Mirjam Knutas. Sometime before 1967, Ms. Knutas was on holiday in the Canary Islands with her mother, when she heard the Lord tell her to go to Korea to

17. Fr. Alberto Ibáñez then had to withdraw at the order of his Jesuit superior, who some years later changed his judgment, and fully supported Fr. Ibáñez's charismatic and ecumenical involvement. The information on Fr. Alberto Ibáñez comes from a personal interview by the author on February 22, 2013.

18. See MacNutt, "Latin America," and Anon., "Retreats."

19. The Bible Study and Prayer Group is the name given to a movement within the Presbyterian Church of Ghana, which became a major disseminator of charismatic renewal. See Omenyo, *Pentecost*, 140–53.

20. Ibid., 104.

introduce the baptism in the Spirit to Catholics. She knew no Catholics at all. After struggling with this word, on the last day of her holiday she asked the Lord for confirmation by arranging for her to encounter a Catholic priest. As she prepared for bed without such an encounter, her mother felt ill and asked Mirjam to go for some medicine. In the pharmacy there was a Catholic priest! So Ms. Knutas went to Korea, but had to wait five years before anything happened. Then a Catholic man in the US military joined her Bible study group, and was baptized in the Spirit. He recommended that a German missionary sister, Sr. Erna Schmid, visit Ms. Knutas, and this sister was baptized in the Spirit in January 1971. Within a month Sr. Erna gathered a group of priests and brothers in the apartment of Ms. Knutas, and others received. Ms. Knutas then arranged a Pentecost weekend in 1971 featuring Archer Torrey, an Episcopal priest and grandson of a famous US evangelist. This weekend, when sixteen people gathered, is celebrated as the birth of the CCR in Korea.[21]

The Ministry of David du Plessis

During these early years of the charismatic movement, David du Plessis (1905–1987), a Pentecostal leader who became widely known as "Mr. Pentecost," played a very important role.[22] Du Plessis, a South African by origin who had lived in the USA since 1948, heard a call of the Lord to witness to the churches about baptism in the Spirit. As du Plessis obeyed this call, he insisted during his global travels that what the churches were now experiencing in the charismatic movement was the same blessing as the Pentecostals had received at Azusa Street in 1906. In this way, he was a key witness to the spiritual affinity of the Pentecostal and charismatic movements. This conviction took David du Plessis to Rome, and that led to the Catholic–Pentecostal dialogue, of which he was the first Pentecostal co-chair.

Conclusion

Evidence indicates that the beginnings of the charismatic movement in the Catholic Church were uncoordinated by human agencies and had the

21. Bro. Deporres Stilp tells this story in "Tenth Anniversary," 4–8. This issue also contains reminiscences from Sr. Erna Schmid and Rev. Archer Torrey.

22. See du Plessis, *Man*. Despite the formation of the David du Plessis Archives at Fuller Theological Seminary, there is still no scholarly study published on his life and ministry.

character of a surprising outbreak. As an unexpected outbreak, there were numerous occurrences that were experienced as a sovereign grace of the Lord. Although the overall movement was not humanly planned, there were many human instruments used by the Lord that significantly included the witness and ministry of charismatic Protestants and Pentecostals. Cardinal Suenens recognized this when he stated clearly, "Historically, this 'awakening' comes to us from classical Pentecostalism, as well as from what is generally termed Neo-pentecostalism."[23]

In the following chapters I reflect on the development of the charismatic renewal, particularly in the Catholic Church, with a focus on its ecumenical expressions. Even though CCR has not maintained its earlier impetus in North America and much of Western Europe, it has become a major force in the churches of Africa, Asia, and Latin America. Although CCR has had its ups and downs over forty-five years, its high points and its low points, its triumphs and its scandals, it is clear that CCR has acquired an accepted status in the Catholic Church, especially through the encouragement of the popes, and the official recognition of International Catholic Charismatic Renewal Services (ICCRS). The Holy Spirit continues to pour out these gifts. This charismatic work of the Spirit continues to take place across the denominational spectrum, and new bridges are being built across the deep divides. The Holy Spirit has not forgotten the ecumenical potential.

23. Suenens, *Ecumenism*, 19. By "neo-Pentecostalism," Suenens was referring to the charismatic movement within the Protestant churches.

2

Catholic Charismatic Renewal as a Fruit of the Second Vatican Council

How is it possible that the charismatic renewal with its origins in Pentecostal and Protestant milieux should be received and welcomed within the Catholic Church? The short answer: Vatican Two. Without the Second Vatican Council, it seems inconceivable that there could have been charismatic renewal in the Catholic Church. A more comprehensive answer would be: it was made possible by the renewing currents gathering momentum in the Catholic Church from the time of Pope Leo XIII (1878–1903), particularly the development of Catholic biblical studies, the liturgical movement, mobilization of the laity, and the first stirrings of the ecumenical movement, all of which were received and officially approved by the Second Vatican Council.

Pentecostal and Evangelical Christians have rarely grasped the importance for God's purposes of this Holy Spirit movement reaching the Catholic Church. To see the phenomenon of Spirit-filled Catholics as the Lord's mercy saving individual believers within a recalcitrant Spirit-resistant institution is not enough. Rather we can see the awakening or renewal of the Catholic Church that is much wider than CCR as one key element in God's strategy to move the whole body of Christ toward the coming consummation. With such a wider vision of God's purposes, the renewing vision and impetus of the Second Vatican Council has major consequences for the entire Christian world. This perspective makes it necessary to understand more clearly the relationship of CCR to the council, and the importance of the council for the revival and renewal of the entire body of Christ.

How Did the Second Vatican Council Prepare the Ground for the Catholic Charismatic Renewal?

Soon after January 1959 when Pope John XXIII announced the calling of the council, he composed a prayer for recitation during the years of its preparation. In this prayer Catholics all over the world were imploring the Lord, "Renew your wonders in this, our day, as by a new Pentecost."[1] Many of the first Catholics caught up in CCR came from student milieux, excited by the debates and decisions of the council. They immediately understood that the charismatic renewal was a wonderful answer of the Lord to the prayer of Pope John.

The Second Vatican Council prepared the way for CCR with its general teaching and emphases, and in some more specific ways. In general, the return to the sources, biblical and patristic, that characterized the work of the council, fostered a Christ-centered understanding of the church, her worship, and her mission, within a clearly Trinitarian presentation of Christian faith. In these developments, aided by the Eastern Catholic bishops and the Orthodox observers, there was a stronger teaching on the role of the Holy Spirit. The Christ-centeredness of the renewal with its accentuation of the Holy Spirit instinctively led the charismatic Catholics to know they were in sync with the renewal mandated by the council. In particular, the teaching on divine revelation, centered on and summed up in the person of Jesus, the incarnate Word, "who is himself both the mediator and the sum total of revelation,"[2] resonated with the experience of the charismatic Catholics.

More specifically, the council texts facilitated the church's openness to the Renewal in a number of ways:

The Teaching on Charisms

During the council, there was a very lively debate on charisms in the life of the church. Interestingly, there were two main protagonists: Cardinal Suenens of Malines, Belgium, who argued that the charisms belong to the normal life of the church in every age, and should be welcomed accordingly, and Cardinal Ernesto Ruffini from Palermo, Sicily, who argued that the charisms belonged to the apostolic age, and are not to be expected today. The position of Cardinal Suenens won the support of the bishops, and found expression in

1. Cited in O'Connor, *Pentecostal Movement*, 287.
2. *DV* 2.

the constitution on the church.[3] Here we find a vision of God's provision for the church that will be more fully developed by John Paul II at Pentecost in 1998. The council added that "whether these charisms be very remarkable or more simple and widely diffused, they are to be received with thanksgiving and consolation." There is then a call for discernment by church authority, whose office is "not . . . to extinguish the Spirit, but to test all things."[4] This paragraph was, we may say, ready made for the Renewal, for while charisms are not restricted to charismatic renewal, it is this renewal that most clearly manifests the range of charisms recorded in the New Testament, in particular the spiritual gifts of 1 Corinthians 12:8–10. Here the renewal illustrates the teaching of St. Paul that charisms are given to each member of the body for the upbuilding of the whole.[5]

The Opening Up of the Bible to All Catholics

The council fathers deliberately put an end to the defensiveness regarding the Bible that had characterized the Catholic Church of the Counter Reformation, along with the suspicion that enthusiastic Bible-reading is inherently Protestant and not really Catholic. So the bishops said: "Access to sacred scripture ought to be widely available to the christian faithful."[6] For the Catholic Church to embrace the charismatic renewal would have been difficult if this opening up of God's Word to all the faithful without restriction had not taken place.

The Teaching on the Laity

Of all the rich teaching on the church in *Lumen Gentium*, the teaching on the laity has been of huge importance and relevance to CCR. The council

---

3. "It is not only through the sacraments and the ministries that the Holy Spirit makes the people holy, leads them and enriches them with his virtues. Allotting his gifts 'at will to each individual' (1 Cor 12:11), he also distributes special graces among the faithful of every rank." *LG* 12.

4. *LG* 12.

5. The widespread Catholic pattern today of referring to the charisms of religious orders and communities is a derivative usage that in strongly "top-down" communities can lead to the exaltation of the charism of the community at the expense of the variety of charisms being given to its members.

6. *DV* 22.

teaches that all the baptized "have been made sharers in their own way in the priestly, prophetic, and kingly office of Christ," and so "the apostolate of the laity is a sharing in the church's saving mission."[7] This teaching made it much easier for the Catholic Church to accept the new roles that laypeople baptized in the Holy Spirit began to exercise within the church. The experience of the renewal confirmed the teaching on the universal call to holiness, as those baptized in the Spirit longed for deeper prayer and union with Christ.[8]

The Acceptance of the Ecumenical Movement

At the Second Vatican Council, in its decree on ecumenism the Catholic Church officially embraced the ecumenical movement in its goal of restoring the full visible unity of the one body of Jesus Christ: "Today, in many parts of the world, under the influence of the grace of the Holy Spirit, many efforts are being made in prayer, word, and action to attain that fullness of unity which Jesus Christ desires. This sacred council, therefore, exhorts all the Catholic faithful to recognize the signs of the times and to take an active and intelligent part in the work of ecumenism."[9] Moreover, for the first time in official Catholic teaching the council taught that the Holy Spirit is present in a salvific way in the other Christian communities of faith: "For the Spirit of Christ has not refrained from using them [the separated churches and communities] as means of salvation which derive their efficacy from the very fullness of grace and truth entrusted to the Catholic Church."[10] Without this recognition, it would have been impossible for the Catholic Church to have welcomed this current of new life, that came not just from on high, but through other Christians.

So in what sense can it be said that Vatican Two was a cause of the charismatic renewal? While the council was not a direct cause of the charismatic renewal, the council clearly played an important preparatory role for Catholics to receive its grace, and for the movement to be welcomed by church authority. Pope John's calling of a council for the renewal of the church introduced the term "renewal" into regular Catholic terminology. This renewal context had two important consequences. First, the council's

7. *LG* 31, 33.
8. Ibid., 39–42.
9. *UR* 4.
10. Ibid., 3.

vision for the renewal of the Catholic Church and its teaching on the church led directly to the first charismatic Catholics understanding that this renewal is for the whole church. This conviction provided a sense of direction for CCR, and led to some strategic thinking on how to permeate the whole church with this refreshing work of the Holy Spirit.[11] Second, the interdenominational character of its origins was interpreted in the light of the council's decree on ecumenism. Just as this movement in the Catholic Church is for the renewal of the Catholic Church, so Catholics understood its interdenominational character as a grace for the unity of the whole body of Christ. Neither of these aspects had a clear parallel in the charismatic movement within the Protestant churches.

What Does Church Renewal Mean?

Inevitably, for all Catholics conciliar renewal was experienced as change—either welcome change or very unwelcome change. For ordinary Catholics not versed in the discussions of the council, Vatican Two meant first of all change in the liturgy. For Catholics in the English-speaking world, that to be honest had contributed little to the conciliar reforms, for which it was generally unprepared, Vatican Two meant the new liturgical forms more than the biblical and liturgical understanding that lay behind them.[12] Liturgical changes were followed by a multiplication of new structures from the full apparatus of episcopal conferences, to diocesan commissions, and parish councils. Patterns of formation changed dramatically, and more and more laypeople played significant roles in Catholic life. Catholics started to recognize the presence and the role of the other Christian communities. The point of this brief resumé is to show how for most Catholics the term renewal came to signify changes in church structure and organization. For the more educated, renewal meant above all the renewal of theology—for the English-speaking world in the twenty years following the council, catching up with the continental scholars, and in more recent times being influenced by new trends in the United States more than by continental European theologians.

11. See, for example, Clark, *Building Christian Communities*, and *Where Are We Headed?*

12. The one contribution from the English-speaking world was the decisive role of bishops and theologians from the United States in the inclusion of the declaration on religious liberty, *Dignitatis Humanae.*

After forty-five years of charismatic renewal, we can say that the charismatic renewal can help the whole church to understand the deeper meaning of all renewal. Of course, church renewal is much wider than charismatic renewal. One would be arrogant and ideological to claim that charismatic renewal is the only authentic form of renewal. Nonetheless, at the heart of this work of God something essential about the heart of church renewal is being demonstrated. This is not primarily a statement about theological theory, but about lived faith experience. Let us try and unpack these lessons about the nature of church renewal.

It Is Totally Christocentric

The experience of renewal is the fruit of Jesus Christ being placed at the center. The Holy Spirit reveals Jesus as Savior and Lord, not just of individuals, but as Savior and Lord of the church. He is teacher of the church, he is the message proclaimed by the church. He is the shepherd and the food; he is Alpha and Omega—for the church and for the whole creation.

It Is Spirit-Led, Spirit-Inspired and Spirit-Directed

The experience of renewal is a schooling in being led and guided by the Holy Spirit, in receiving light from the Holy Spirit to understand the Scriptures, and to receive guidance for all forms of ministry and service. As a gift to the church, the renewal can demonstrate what it means for church leadership to be inspired, led, and directed by the Holy Spirit.

It Is Totally Biblical

The experience of renewal is being drawn into the Word of God, in being saturated in the Word, in submitting our human patterns of thinking to the ways of the Lord whose judgments are "unsearchable" and whose ways are "inscrutable" (see Rom 11:33). The experience of renewal helps to open us up to "the mystery of Christ," that is at the center of the biblical revelation, the mystery of Christ, that is the one plan of God from before all creation, that is made manifest by the coming of Christ, and that is revealed to the saints by the Holy Spirit (see Rom 16:25–26; Eph 1:9–10; 3:4–5; Col 1:26–27).

It is Worshipful and Gives Glory to God

All authentic renewal comes from the Holy Spirit who is poured into our hearts. Jesus said about the Holy Spirit, "He will glorify me, for he will take what is mine and declare it to you" (John 16:14). Renewal in the Holy Spirit will orient our hearts and minds to God, issuing in revitalized worship nourished by regular personal prayer. So all authentic renewal will place worship more clearly at the center of all church life; it will intensify the ways in which the liturgy and prayer together influence our ministry and outreach, as well as the ways they feed back into liturgy and prayer.

It is Evangelistic

Renewal in the Holy Spirit not only enthuses the believer, but also gives a personal testimony to share. Authentic renewal will issue in evangelism, not just by a trained elite, but by ordinary Christians speaking of the Lord whom they have come to know and to love.

It is Dialogical and Not Judgmental

Besides the proclamation of Jesus, authentic renewal leads to an openness to dialogue. Dialogue should not weaken evangelistic witness and mission. Renewal can purify our proclamation of the gospel by eliminating all elements that try to promote the church by denigration of the others. With the others—other Christians, other religions, other cultures—it seeks dialogue and discussion.[13] It listens so as to understand. It refuses *a priori* judgments of others without any listening. In relation to other Christians, it seeks to identify the work of the Holy Spirit among them, personally and corporately.

It is Deeply Transformative

The renewing work of the Holy Spirit transforms from within, changing hearts, and conferring new energy for the kingdom of God. In Ezekiel's prophecy of the new covenant era, the Lord promised, "A new heart I will

13. This dialogical pattern is reflected in the pope's decision, following the council, to establish such structures as the Pontifical Council for the Promotion of the Unity of Christians, Pontifical Council for Inter-religious Dialogue, and Pontifical Council for Culture.

give you, and a new spirit I will put within you; and I will take out of your flesh the heart of stone and give you a heart of flesh" (Ezek 36:26). Renewal is not a call to moral improvement, but an opening of our hearts to the Holy Spirit for transformation. This transformation is not limited to churchly spheres of life, but to all human activities in the world as well as in the church.

The Importance for Ecumenism

That the charismatic renewal reveals something vital about the nature of all church renewal itself has major ecumenical significance. Its strongly ecclesial vision enables CCR at its best to combine deep personal transformation with the renewal of corporate life in liturgy, catechesis, pastoral care, and social outreach. As an interdenominational phenomenon with its roots in Evangelical and Pentecostal revivals, it has the potential to be a real bridge between the churches committed to an ecumenical vision, and the Evangelical–Pentecostal world that has kept its distance from the ecumenical movement with its deep suspicion of all that is institutional. With its spiritual affinity to the Pentecostal world and the wider charismatic movement, and its enthusiastic reception of Vatican Two, CCR has an unparalleled opportunity to demonstrate the character of authentic ecumenism as explained in the conciliar decree: "There can be no ecumenism worthy of the name without interior conversion."[14]

The great potential of CCR to help the wider Pentecostal-charismatic world to understand the whole movement's potential for Christian unity is based on this combination of its strong ecclesial sense, its greater coherence as a movement, its size, and its global extent. But for this potential to be realized, the leaders and people of CCR have to understand its ecumenical origins and character, and to build bridges to the Holy Spirit currents in other churches, and to the Pentecostals. This process requires a willingness to work through the suspicions and the opposition, and to learn from the work of the Spirit among the others. In their very different ways the Second Vatican Council and CCR have changed the Christian world scenery. They have created the situation in which it is possible to imagine a coming together of the historic church world represented by the Catholic Church, and all the revival streams of the Evangelical and Pentecostal worlds. Without the Second Vatican Council, CCR would not have been possible. Without CCR, there would be no sustainable bridge between these two worlds.

14. *UR* 7.

Without CCR, the Catholic Church would have difficulty receiving the work of the Holy Spirit among the Pentecostals and the Evangelicals. Without the council behind CCR, the Evangelical–Pentecostal world cannot begin to look at the gifts the Lord wants to give them through the Catholic Church.

3

The Newness of the Work of the Holy Spirit

THE WORK OF THE Holy Spirit is always new, for the Holy Spirit is the Creator God. The Holy Spirit never simply repeats what has been done before. The Holy Spirit does not produce clones or automated systems. There is a continuity in the work of the Holy Spirit, but the creativity of the Spirit is always evident. Jesus said of the Holy Spirit: "he will take what is mine and declare it to you" (John 16:15). This statement holds together the never-changing foundation in Jesus Christ, and the creative life-giving role of the Holy Spirit. The Spirit's role is manifested differently in the liturgical-sacramental ministry that is continuous, and in the work of God in the charismatic dimension of the church that is wholly unpredictable.[1] The creative character of the Holy Spirit is most evident in all these unexpected outpourings from above, of which the modern charismatic movement is a striking example. There is a remarkable newness in this work of the Holy Spirit. This does not mean that such elements have never been known before in the history of the church. But the present forms manifest a newness that have their own hallmark, and that can be recognized as a particular grace for our time. In this chapter we will look at some of the remarkable examples of newness for church life that characterize the charismatic renewal.

---

1. See chapter 10 on the distinction between the institutional and the charismatic dimensions of the church.

The Charisms

The charismatic renewal has been marked by the restoration of the spiritual gifts listed by the apostle Paul in 1 Corinthians 12:8–10. Of these perhaps the most noteworthy are the gift of prophecy, gifts of healing, and speaking in other tongues. Is the form taken by these gifts in the renewal identical to what Paul had known? Almost certainly not. They are the same fundamental gifts—and so Paul's teaching on the charisms remains fully relevant—but with the characteristic creativity of the Holy Spirit, they take forms today that are new, and that express the wisdom of God for our day.

Perhaps what is most obviously new, at least since the earliest days of the church, is the outpouring of charisms on all Christian flesh, not just rarely, but all the time, not just on the ascetic striving for holiness, but on the ordinary Christian. With the exception of speaking in tongues, the exercise of these charisms associated with the renewal draws the recipients into the sphere of ministering the blessings of the Lord to others. This feature has in many ways transformed the life of the church where the renewal has flourished, and it has not been seen as peripheral, or even pushed to the margins.

The renewal is restoring prophetic utterance to the consciousness of the church. This is not saying that nothing spoken outside the sphere of charismatic renewal can be prophetic. That is obviously not true. But the awareness of prophecy as a charism promised to the Christian community is new for the Catholic Church of recent centuries, as it is new for the churches of the Reformation. Are the forms taken by prophetic utterance the same as in New Testament times? Almost certainly not. Here again there is a creativity of the Holy Spirit, that is both addressing the deepest needs of the church today, and that is taking on flesh in contemporary forms. Because prophetic utterance was not part of regular Christian experience, the prophetic activities of the Spirit require a training in the prophetic: forming the expectation that the Lord will speak to his people, teaching them how to hear the Lord, how to sift the word of the Lord from our own inner voices and from our biases and inclinations, giving the courage to speak out what has been received. Similarly, a learning is necessary in how to receive prophetic words, how to discern them, what to highlight, and what to allow the Holy Spirit to fructify without our embellishment. This experience of the prophetic raises our expectations about the whole work of the Holy Spirit in the church, which in turn makes our prayer bolder, and heightens our attentiveness to the action of God in the church and in the world.

Again the renewal has brought experience of the gifts of healing, an area in which no priest, religious, or layperson had been trained. Fr. Rufus Pereira from India (1933–2012), who became one of the best-known Catholic teachers on the ministry of healing and deliverance, spoke of his total surprise at God using him in this ministry about which seminary training had remained silent. Along with many others in CCR, as Fr. Rufus began to pray for the sick and diseased, the Holy Spirit was not only the agent but also their teacher. They learned by experience that there is not one gift of healing given identically to many, but many "gifts of healing" (1 Cor 12:9), which have something basic in common, but take very different forms. When the Pentecostals promoted the ministry of healing, the focus was on physical healing. But with the renewal in the Catholic and Anglican Churches, attention was also paid to "inner healing," the healing of emotions. This again was distinctively new. This development represented the reception of these gifts by the more middleclass and educated public to whom many Catholics and Anglicans were ministering, as well as the knowledge of modern psychology, and a growing awareness of the psychosomatic character of many illnesses.

Another obvious example of a newness is the gift of speaking in other tongues. While charismatic Christians do not see tongues as a *sine qua non* for Christian life, this gift would seem to have a bigger place in the renewal than it had in the New Testament church. To recognize this is in no way a criticism of the renewal for departure from the apostolic origins; it is to see a particular expression of the wisdom of God for the church today. For we live in a society and a church, at least in the West, that has become very rationalistic, expecting to understand and explain everything. We have become very utilitarian, seeing no point in anything without a functional payoff. All these attitudes cause the making of unintelligible sounds to seem particularly ridiculous. One could say with a little exaggeration that praying in tongues is of great heavenly benefit, but of no earthly use. But the experience of this unintelligible prayer enables Christians to express their deepest longings and instincts to the Lord beyond what they are capable of articulating. In this way, this gift speaks to a particular need of the contemporary church.

Praise and Worship

The creativity of the Holy Spirit has been very evident in the sphere of praise and worship. To be filled with the Holy Spirit is to be filled with the praise of God: "O Lord, open thou my lips, and my mouth shall show forth thy praise" (Ps 51:15). The charismatic renewal has been marked by spontaneous praise issuing from the lips of those baptized in the Spirit. Sometimes this takes the form of whole groups raising their voices to God simultaneously, often in tongues, but also in biblical language, and in our own words. The coming of the Spirit has always raised hearts and voices to the Lord, but the patterns emerging in the renewal have their own character and significance.

This creativity has led to a vast new repertoire of songs and choruses, many of them the setting of biblical passages and imagery to music. Although the quality of the new songs varies considerably, there are many that reflect the beauty and the depth of the Holy Spirit. This creativity has also blessed the wider church, for songs and choruses of the renewal are now widely used in Christian worship, liturgical and non liturgical, with many Christians having no idea of their provenance.[2] As this creativity of the Spirit extends to people being freed to express their love of the Lord through their bodies and through physical gestures (e.g., in upraised arms and in hand-clapping) it has also set their feet free to dance, and to move in procession for the Lord. Again some forms of sacred dance have been incorporated into Christian worship in the past, but the renewal with its openness to bodily expression has produced new forms of dance, mime, and artistic creativity. The present-day forms reflect both the creativity of the human spirit open to the Holy Spirit, and particular aspects of contemporary culture.

New Forms of Community Life

The charismatic renewal, especially in the Catholic Church, has given rise to distinctively new forms of community life. The Catholic tradition has a long history of intentional communities, but they have been monastic

---

2. The new charismatic groupings, earlier often called nondenominational, have especially shown a creativity in charismatic music. Thus, hymns, songs, and choruses from such sources are now widely sung within most church traditions. These include the works from Vineyard musicians (Brian Doerksen, David Ruis), from Hillsong (Darlene Zschech), and others such as Graham Kendrick, Dave Fellingham, and Chris Bowater.

or mission-oriented celibate communities of those who take vows of poverty, chastity, and obedience. The few prior examples of intentional communities with married couples and families were typically rather eccentric and short-lived. With the dynamism of the Holy Spirit, many baptized in the Spirit have felt the call to form community, or to join a community, sometimes but not always inspired and led by a founder-figure, often a layperson.[3]

There has been great diversity in the new patterns of community developing within the renewal, particularly after the first phase when many in the English-speaking world wanted to copy the North American covenant communities, especially the Word of God at Ann Arbor, Michigan. One major contrast among the larger communities is between the more urban, evangelistic, and formation-oriented, on the one hand,[4] and the more rural and monastic, or contemplative, on the other hand.[5] Another difference is between communities focusing on serving the church in many aspects of life, often virtually as wide as diocesan and parish life, generally with lifelong commitment as the goal or ideal,[6] and communities primarily focused on a particular ministry, such as evangelism, family life, or serving the poor.[7] Some new charismatic communities are completely celibate, and represent a charismatic pattern of consecrated life.

The new charismatic communities have often developed new forms of communal living and mutual engagement, seeking how to develop patterns of profound faith-sharing, while respecting the commitments and demands of family life. For example, many urban communities have developed patterns of clustering, whereby families buy or rent homes in the same neighborhood, so as to facilitate a shared life. In some larger communities with a

---

3. Virtually all the North American covenant communities were founded by laypeople; the Emmanuel community in Paris was founded by Pierre Goursat, now being proposed as a candidate for beatification, and Martine Lafitte; the Emmanuel community in Brisbane and most of the Australian communities had lay founders, as had the Light of Christ community in Kota Kinabulu, East Malaysia.

4. For example, the North American covenant communities: in Europe the Emmanuel community and the Chemin Neuf Community, both of French origin; and Koinonia Giovanni Battista, originating in Italy; and in Brazil the community Canção Nova.

5. For example, the community of the Béatitudes from France.

6. The urban, evangelistic, and formation-oriented communities mentioned in the first paragraph of this section (New Forms of Community Life) typically fit into this pattern.

7. The Sion community in England and Ireland is primarily geared towards evangelism, and has members who come just for a number of years.

number of priest members, the close relationships of priests and laypeople all making a communal engagement, provides new models for priestly and lay collaboration, and the overcoming of inherited forms of clericalism.

Teaching

The charismatic renewal has given rise to new patterns of Christian teaching. This has been less remarked upon than the new patterns of worship. What characterizes these new forms of teaching? We have been accustomed to the teaching of doctrine, and what in Britain has been called RE (religious education). We have been used to various patterns of preaching, from mission-type sermons to liturgical homilies, and less happily the mere airing of the priest's favorite ideas. But in the renewal the felt need for very practical and biblical teaching on how to live out the life in the Spirit has been accompanied by God's provision of excellent new teachers, who are mostly laypeople. At the start of the renewal, this form of teaching was given in all the covenant communities, with a major role being played by the Word of God community at Ann Arbor, Michigan, as can be seen from a magazine they produced, *Pastoral Renewal*.[8] Other examples include the Paul, Philip, and John courses promoted by José Prado Flores in Mexico, and the Koinonia Giovanni Battista community, as well as the Cana course, run by the Chemin Neuf community. In many countries the bishops accepted this kind of teaching by laypeople, probably because it was not primarily dogmatic or moral teaching, but something much more practical, somewhere in between religious education and pastoral counseling.

There are evident reasons why this form of teaching flourishes in the new communities: a clearer articulation of their needs from the membership, particularly the married people with young children; the pastoral experience of those seeking to serve them; the possibility of committed communities funding full-time leaders with the time to study and to develop courses; and the deeper commitment needed to support ongoing courses and regular attendance. The new patterns of teaching are primarily a lay creation and reflect various aspects of contemporary society: modern communications; new teaching techniques, including the use of power points, of visual aids and sound clips; and the effectiveness of cell groups.

---

8. *Pastoral Renewal* was published from 1976, being renamed *Faith and Renewal* in 1990, but ceasing publication in 1992.

New Forms of Evangelization

The outpouring of the Holy Spirit in the charismatic renewal generates a desire to evangelize, and to spread the blessings that have been received. Those baptized in the Spirit will experience the power of the Spirit at work in others as they proclaim the word of the gospel. Through the renewal, the laity as well as the clergy is mobilized for this proclamation. For this reason, the renewal is a major resource for the church in responding to the call of John Paul II and of Benedict XVI for a New Evangelization.

The creativity of the Holy Spirit is evident in various new patterns of evangelization that have sprung up in the renewal. Various forms of coordinated street evangelism have been pioneered; for example, the Emmanuel community in Paris, France. The Alpha course, that has had an immense effect throughout the world, was developed within the renewed Anglican parish of Holy Trinity, Brompton, in London, England, and is now spreading the fastest in the Catholic Church with strong encouragement from many bishops. This is another development that was unimaginable merely twenty or twenty-five years ago.[9] Others have pioneered healing on the streets, and street prayer ministry, as new forms of evangelization for urban and city situations.

Deliverance Ministry

The manifestation of the Spirit in the charismatic renewal not only makes visible the work of the Holy Spirit of God, but it also exposes the spirits of darkness. Here we can see the same pattern that was so evident in the public ministry of Jesus. When Jesus teaches with authority in the synagogue, a man with an unclean spirit cries out, "What have you to do with us, Jesus of Nazareth? Have you come to destroy us? I know who you are, the Holy One of God!" (Mark 1:23–24). The manifestation of evil spirits requires a response in the name of Jesus, and the power of the Spirit.

So we find everywhere in the renewal the practice of deliverance ministry, and the rise of people with a sense of calling to deliverance ministry.[10] The spread of secularism, much noted, has been accompanied by the rise

---

9. See also chapter 6 for more on the Alpha course.

10. Besides Fr. Rufus Pereira, other Catholics who have acquired a reputation for deliverance ministry include Myles Dempsey (Liverpool, England); Fr. Richard McAlear (USA); and Fr. Elias Vella, OFM Conv. (Malta).

of neo-paganism, much less noted, and an increased fascination with the occult, that is evident in any secular bookstore. As a result, more and more people engaged in praying for others are encountering manifestations of disturbance as the unholy is confronted by the holy. While deliverance from evil forces has always been present in the church, the emerging patterns are distinctively new: in the rise of ministries specializing in deliverance, in deliverance becoming a common occurrence, in a clearer distinction between deliverance and solemn exorcism, and in the participation of laypeople in deliverance ministry.[11]

The Ministry and Empowerment of All the Baptized

In all these developments we can see the mobilization and empowering of the laity, as well as a renewal in the ministry and service of priests and religious. We can see the laity entering into the mission into which they were initiated at their baptism, as *Lumen Gentium* teaches. The vision of a church, in which every member plays an active and constructive part, is brought alive before our eyes. This contemporary work of the Spirit corresponds to the vision of the church as the body of Christ presented by the apostle Paul in the first letter to the Corinthians: "To each is given the manifestation of the Spirit for the common good" (1 Cor 12:7). Then follows the list of spiritual gifts that characterize the Pentecostal and charismatic movements. And after this list, he continues: "All these are inspired by one and the same Spirit, who apportions to each one individually as he wills. For just as the body is one and has many members, and all the members of the body, though many, are one body, so it is with Christ" (1 Cor 12:11–12).

The Newness of the Holy Spirit and Christian Unity

All the instances of the creativity of the Holy Spirit in bringing forth new patterns and forms of ministry and service to God, to the church, and to the world have a major ecumenical significance. First, the ecumenical character and expressions of the charismatic renewal are themselves another striking example of the creativity of the Holy Spirit. But, secondly, all the various instances of creativity have themselves an ecumenical significance. In most

11. "The solemn exorcism, called 'a major exorcism,' can be performed only by a priest and with the permission of the bishop." *CCC* 1673. When *The Code of Canon Law* speaks of exorcism of "the possessed" it is referring to solemn exorcism. *CCL* 1172 §1.

of the instances (e.g., the charisms, praise and worship, new forms of evangelization) there is a parallel creativity in the renewal movement in other Christian communions and in the "nondenominational" expressions. It is this commonality that makes possible a sharing in these forms of Christian life with other Christians baptized in the Spirit, and that may represent the clearest example to date of what John Paul II said about ecumenical dialogue that it "is not just the exchange of ideas, but an exchange of gifts."[12]

Of major significance for the unity of the church is the spread of the charismatic movement to young Jews in the messianic Jewish movement, which spread from California under the influence of the Jesus movement from 1967. These young Jewish converts were adamant that they remained Jews after their acceptance of Jesus, and were determined to live as Jewish disciples of Jesus. The explosive power of this outpouring of the Spirit provided the main dynamism for the rise of the contemporary messianic Jewish movement with a remarkable creativity of the Spirit in new songs—mostly based on the Old Testament Scriptures—and dances. Its presence was made known to other charismatic Christians at the Kansas City Conference of 1977, where the messianic Jews had their own teaching and worship track. Although the focus of many messianic Jews is the consolidation and spread of their Jewish faith in Jesus, their significance for Christian unity is twofold: first, by helping all the churches return to the sources in Israel; and second, by recalling the churches to the fact that the original unity of the church was the ingrafting of Gentiles into the body of Jewish believers (see Rom 11:17–24; Eph 2:14–16; 3:4–6).[13]

The Creativity of the Holy Spirit within the Church of History

In most of the examples of a genuine newness given above, the newness represents new patterns, and new forms of exercise within ministries and forms of life that have always existed. So Christian worship has always involved praise of God, but it is unlikely to have previously taken the form of corporate charismatic praise as we know it today. The ministry

---

12. *UUS* 28.

13. After the charismatic consultation in Viviers, France, in 1973, a specialist in Jewish relations, Père Georges Maurice wrote: "For us [Catholics and Protestants] Israel is revealing [in French: un révélateur] . . . because the break with Israel was the original break [source-rupture], the type of all the other divisions that have occurred throughout history." Viviers, 140.

of the church has always been a teaching ministry, but now there are new patterns of practical teaching, often given by lay leaders, that are new. There has always been a preaching of the gospel of salvation, but there is something new in the forms being taken by evangelization in the renewal, and in who is doing it. There has always been community life in the church, but the forms being taken in charismatic communities represent a genuine newness. Likewise there has always been the ministry of exorcism, but the forms being taken today in the ministry of deliverance are without a precise precedent.

What would seem to be without any precedent in previous centuries is the ecumenical character of the charismatic renewal. Just as ecumenism was new for the Catholic Church at the Second Vatican Council, so the forms of interdenominational sharing introduced by the charismatic renewal are new and without precedent. The argument sometimes heard that ecumenism is not new in the life of the church, because there were earlier efforts to heal church divisions, is not persuasive. It is not simply that any fruit from those efforts was short-lived. It is that the fundamental thinking of the council's decree on ecumenism is new in the history of the church: that unity requires renewal and repentance, that the Holy Spirit is at work in the other Christian confessions, that respectful dialogue between separated communities is essential, that there are degrees of communion. Here the creativity of the Spirit in theological rethinking makes possible the acceptance of the creativity of the Spirit in the wider life of the church.

4

The Challenges of the Renewal

ALL THE NEW EXPRESSIONS arising from the Holy Spirit's work in the Renewal pose challenges of varying extent and intensity to the Christian Church as a whole. In an interdenominational movement of the Spirit, some challenges are greater to the Catholic Church, some are greater for historic Protestants, and some are greater for the free churches. There is always and inescapably a challenge. The overall challenges are equally great for all Christian traditions, but the points where the challenges bite will vary.

This posing of many challenges should not be seen as a problem. It belongs to the very character of initiatives of the Holy Spirit. First, the coming of the Holy Spirit immediately challenges all that is not holy, all that is not worthy of the Lord. The greater the move of the Spirit and the more extensive its scale: the bigger the challenge. Second, the coming of the Holy Spirit reveals something of God's purposes. This necessarily uncovers the truth of the word of the Lord to the prophet Isaiah: "For my thoughts are not your thoughts, neither are your ways my ways, says the Lord. For as the heavens are higher than the earth, so are my ways higher than your ways and my thoughts than your thoughts" (55:8–9). The sovereign moves of the Holy Spirit expose our all too human thinking, and raise our gaze to the divine level.[1]

---

1. Apart from a passing reference, I do not cover here the challenges posed by the messianic Jewish movement, which is largely charismatic. This is primarily because the charismatic movement as a whole has paid little attention to the messianic Jewish movement, and so is largely unaware of its potential significance. I have treated these challenges in Hocken, *Challenges*.

Some of the Challenges

The overarching challenge common to all the particular challenges posed by the charismatic renewal to the churches is the relationship of the new to the old. Whenever new patterns arise within the church, questions arise as to their relationship to older patterns and received traditions. While the focus in this chapter is on the Catholic Church, similar issues are raised in other churches, particularly the Anglican and the Lutheran. A hallmark of CCR from the beginning is that its leaders have understood that the distinctive gifts of the renewal have to be received into the centuries-long heritage of the church, from which also they have constantly to receive. This conviction that the renewal was an answer to Pope John's prayer for a new Pentecost, and was a God-given fruit of the Second Vatican Council, gave the first charismatic Catholics a deep confidence that this reception of the new into the old would indeed take place. This confidence enabled Catholics not to be perturbed by a much-publicized prophecy from a Pentecostal source in the 1970s that the Catholic Church would reject CCR.

The reception of a new and charismatic work of the Holy Spirit into the age-long tradition, itself preserved, guided, and protected by the Holy Spirit, is much more than adaptation of the ways things are done in the church. Because the Holy Spirit is the Creator, every work of the Holy Spirit in the church is creative of new life. Simply rearranging structures cannot by itself produce new life. It can lead to greater efficiency and better communications, but it will not engender new life. The Lord, who is breathing this renewal upon the church, is like the householder "who brings out of his treasure what is new and what is old" (Matt 13:52). The Father's treasure is Jesus Christ, and all the work of the Holy Spirit reveals more of the Lord Jesus and his ways.

The common element in these challenges is the interaction of the charismatic and the institutional, between what the Holy Spirit does unexpectedly and what belongs to the permanent basic heritage of the church, which will be examined later, in chapter 10. Here my focus is on the points of challenge, where the new knocks at the door of the old. While the whole conciliar renewal flowing from the Second Vatican Council is challenging for the church, and itself has a charismatic character,[2] CCR poses major challenges in a more obvious way because the renewal manifests the char-

2. See address of John Paul II, Meeting with Ecclesial Movements and New Communities, at Pentecost 1998. (Website link in bibliography.) We examine this contribution further in chapter 10.

acter of the charismatic more strongly precisely as a "charismatic renewal." In the same way, all authentic renewal comes from the Holy Spirit, and as such has a creative character, so the renewal as charismatic renewal manifests the creativity of the Holy Spirit in a strikingly visible way.[3]

The Worship of the Church

The Renewal is a movement that loves to worship the Lord. From the beginning, its characteristic meetings were prayer meetings in which praise of the Lord was central. You can have a charismatic prayer meeting without prayer ministry, and you can have a charismatic prayer meeting without a teaching, even though prayer ministry and teaching are important elements in most meetings. But you cannot really have a charismatic prayer meeting without any corporate praise of the Lord. But for charismatic Catholics, the heart of the church's worship is the liturgy, an emphasis insisted on by the Second Vatican Council and more clearly manifested by the liturgical reforms since the council. So the charismatic Catholic is immediately confronted by the need to receive the gift of charismatic praise into the liturgical tradition.

The praise of God as lived in the renewal is clearly holistic, involving the whole person (body, emotions and affections, spirit) actively expressed in corporate worship. Here the charismatic Catholic quickly discovers that this praise is actually at the center of liturgical worship, but it can now be lived more fully, as more levels within the worshiping believer are actively engaged. This experience has been received by those in the renewal as a living out of the "active participation" in the liturgy presented by the council fathers as a goal of liturgical renewal. "To develop active participation, the people should be encouraged to take part by means of acclamations, responses, psalms, antiphons, hymns, as well as by actions, gestures, and bodily attitudes."[4]

The challenge to bring the charismatic and the liturgical together is common to the whole renewal in the Catholic Church. How it is done can vary from place to place, and from community to community. Almost everywhere, there are charismatic meetings that are distinct from the liturgy. This serves the purpose of growing in the gift of charismatic praise, and of developing the exercise of the charisms. But equally the need is everywhere

3. See chapter 3 for examples of the creativity of the Spirit in the renewal.

4. *SC* 30; see also paras. 14, 21, 26–27, 50.

felt for a liturgical practice that integrates charismatic creativity into the liturgy in a way that respects its fundamental character. Commonly, this involves (a) having times of extended praise (e.g., at the start of the Mass, perhaps at the Gloria, singing in the Spirit after the consecration, more praise after the communion, and certainly at the end); (b) participants having the freedom to raise their arms and hands, to clap their hands, perhaps to perform a simple dance; and (c) to have a longer teaching during the homily. The experience of "charismatic liturgy" involves discovery of how filled with the Spirit the liturgy already is, with the centrality of praise and thanksgiving, and with the double epiclesis invoked over the bread and the wine, and over the participants in the liturgical action.[5] It also introduces into church practice a new experience of freedom within structure, and the need to learn the difference between creativity within the structure and an abuse of freedom that ignores or operates against the structure. The Holy Spirit teaches us that a worshipful celebration of the liturgy requires more than exact attention to the rubrics, and that it requires a deep respect for the tradition and the structures that have come down through the ages.

The importance of this interaction of the charismatic and the liturgical for the whole Christian world is underlined by the currents of dissatisfaction within the Pentecostal and Evangelical worlds with a constant mixture of songs, preaching, and ministry lacking any biblical or historical structure. This interaction inevitably faces the messianic Jews, who have mostly inherited Evangelical-charismatic patterns, as they seek to develop patterns that are authentically Jewish—for Judaism is a liturgical faith.

The Roles of the Laity and of the Ordained

The Renewal is a transforming movement, as baptism in the Spirit is a transforming occurrence in the life of the believer. And in very obvious ways, the renewal has been transformative for Catholic laypeople. Through being baptized in the Spirit, people are transformed into being active worshipers, very conscious of the privilege of responding to the gift of the Holy Spirit. But these laypeople then begin to serve others in prayer ministry, in counseling, and in giving teachings. The exercise of the spiritual gifts of prophecy and of healing, for example, introduces laypeople into spheres of church life that are experienced as forms of ministry. In the many new communities that belong to the renewal, these forms of lay service and ministry

5. Epiclesis refers to the invocation of the Holy Spirit.

are more marked, as the larger communities are able to support laypeople who work full-time in the service of the Lord. An important instance of these new forms of lay activity is in the area of practical teaching, which is treated in a separate section below.

It is important to see these developments as a grace, and not primarily as a problem. There is a big challenge here, but challenges are not just problems; they are opportunities. The challenge is to rethink the relationship between ordained ministries and forms of ministry open to all the baptized. The more conservative reaction that seeks to limit the word "ministry" to the ordained is too restrictive, and fails to recognize what has been happening without great fuss for over forty years. We can trust in faith that this rethinking will deepen our appreciation for the ordained ministry and its essential role, while purifying the church of forms of clericalism that block the full contribution of the laity.

Preaching, Teaching, and Pastoral Formation

Preaching, teaching, and pastoral formation are important areas for understanding more clearly the difference between ordained ministry and the active service of laypeople that is grounded in their baptism, and that introduces them into the mission of the church. There have obviously been huge developments in Catholic practice since the council, with the restoration of the adult catechumenate, the spread of lay catechists, the use of lectors and eucharistic ministers in the liturgy, and the widespread appointment of youth ministers. But the renewal has widened the scope for such ministry, and opened up some new areas.

One feature of charismatic renewal that has not received enough attention is the rise of new forms of teaching that are different both from liturgical and missional preaching, and from the patterns of religious teaching in school. The key difference is that with the new forms of teaching within the renewal, the goal is the spiritual growth and accompaniment of those being taught. In this respect, this teaching is nearest to catechesis. But it differs from most catechesis in its strongly practical character, and in containing less Catholic jargon. The need for such teaching arose directly from the experience of the Holy Spirit. Through their immersion in the Spirit, people have a new desire for holiness, a desire to grow, and to be formed in the ways of the Lord. The traditional Catholic patterns of instruction did not meet this need, being more oriented to imparting doctrinal truth, and to equipping Catholics to defend themselves against the attacks of Protestants and nonbelievers.

Within the charismatic communities, the leaders have in fact been performing a teaching and a pastoring function. The teaching and the pastoring have been closely linked, for the teaching has been developed to meet evident pastoral needs. Here again, there is a major challenge, because Catholics have reserved the language of pastoring for the ordained ministers. However, rather than classify this as another problem in the renewal, we can see it as the Holy Spirit blessing the church with gifts, that can be a source of renewal for the ordained pastors. There is an encouragement here to pursue in greater depth the real distinction in teaching between ordained and lay ministry. The key difference would seem to lie in the celebration of the "mysteries," within which the preaching-teaching is the breaking open of the Word in the context of the liturgy.

The Encounter with Evil

A major area of challenge arises from the encounter with the powers of evil following a real outpouring of the Holy Spirit. It is a mark of the depth of the Western Church's need for renewal that large sections of both clergy and laity have had no consciousness of the need for ministries of exorcism and deliverance, with many dismissing Satan and evil spirits as merely mythological. But the experience of charismatic renewal has necessitated pastoral responses to the manifestation of evil spirits. This experience raises big questions about much current pastoral practice, and in particular the danger of substituting psychology for spiritual discernment. In the Catholic renewal, where our theology teaches us to respect the order of creation as well as that of redemption, we have to learn how to distinguish the spiritual from the psychic, forms of psychiatric disorder from spiritual oppression or possession.[6]

In consequence of this renewed encounter with the forces of darkness, to distinguish the ministry of deliverance from that of exorcism becomes imperative. In Catholic law, only a priest duly delegated by the bishop can lawfully "exorcise the possessed."[7] "Exorcism is directed at the expulsion of demons or to the liberation from demonic possession through the spiritual

6. See *CCC* 1673.
7. *CCL* 1172.

authority which Jesus entrusted to his Church."[8] By contrast, deliverance addresses forms of molestation or oppression by evil spirits that fall short of possession. Possession normally results only from a deliberate self-giving or consecration to Satan, such as occurs in some forms of witchcraft. The oppression of evil spirits that requires the ministry of deliverance typically results from a history of unrepented sin that opens a person to evil influences, or from an exposure to the realm of the occult.

Ecumenical Sharing

Precisely because the charismatic renewal is the first movement that has equally impacted both Protestants and Catholics, it has given rise to more extended forms of mutual sharing: in worship, in teaching, and in ministry. Because few Catholics have as detailed a knowledge of the Scriptures as Protestants, especially Evangelical pastors, many CCR gatherings have benefited from their biblical teaching. Also in some new areas where charismatic Catholics at first had minimal experience, they found the greater experience of some Protestant teachers very helpful, for example in the realm of spiritual gifts. So, in the early years of the renewal, Protestant teachers with a respect for Catholics were appreciated speakers at major Catholic renewal conferences.

The ecumenical character of the renewal has produced many new pastoral situations and opportunities challenging our received Catholic ways of thinking and operating. This is evident in all charismatic groups with a mixed Catholic–Protestant composition. But the challenges are greatest in ecumenical communities, which have arisen as a fruit of the interchurch dimension of the charismatic experience. Many young Christians baptized in the Spirit, and enjoying close fellowship with Christians of other traditions, had a strong desire to form ecumenical community, so that their shared life in the Spirit could be made the basis of a structured life together. Their leaders were often motivated by a vision of the ecumenical gift of the renewal making a direct contribution to the unity of the body of Christ.

Communities that are ecumenical desire to relate rightly and constructively to the churches or denominations of their members. This marks them out from independent charismatic assemblies, that are not under

---

8. *CCC* 1673. A distinction is made between "solemn exorcism" that requires special delegation from the bishop and other forms of exorcism, as for example the exorcisms within the rite of baptism.

higher-level church authority, or that are under one charismatic leader, perhaps called an apostle. But forming ecumenical community means relating to more than one church authority or leadership, and perhaps several. Another challenge in ecumenical community arises from the need for all members to receive teaching and pastoral care from the ministers of their respective churches, and how to relate this to the teaching and formation provided for all members within the ecumenical community. These questions touch on the difficult issue of identity, including the relationship between denominational or ecclesial identity and Christian identity.[9]

The challenges arising from the ecumenical character of the renewal should not be seen as just one more challenge arising from the charismatic movement. The ecumenical challenge is the overarching challenge that expresses the coherence of all these pastoral and theological challenges. In each area of new initiative and corresponding challenge there is a major ecumenical issue. In the area of worship, the relationship between inherited liturgy and free expression is a major difference between the historic churches and the free churches. Progress in integrating the old and the new here can have major healing consequences for ecumenical relations, particularly between the ancient liturgical churches and the fast-growing Evangelical, Pentecostal, and new charismatic assemblies. The issue is similar with preaching and teaching, and the closely related question of the relationship between the lay and the ordained.

Whenever the Holy Spirit causes new patterns to emerge, that break the rigidity of earlier molds, there is great ecumenical potential. The same applies to ministries of exorcism and deliverance, where there is a wealth of practical experience in the free Pentecostal and charismatic sector. For although these milieux have known patterns of serious abuse, they have also given more attention to the problems arising from these ministries. These examples confirm how fundamental the ecumenical dimension is to the whole charismatic movement, and to its interaction with the Catholic Church and with all the churches.

Ultimately, the experience of the Spirit in renewal challenges Christians from all traditions to understand and value the whole work of God in each church body and tradition as God's gift. The Holy Spirit changes our hearts so that we experience our fellow Christians from other churches as sisters and brothers in the Lord. We become aware of how the Holy Spirit has gifted them, often in different ways from ourselves. So ecumenism will

9. See chapter 8.

mean being challenged first to identify, then to acknowledge, and lastly to receive the gifts represented by the other.[10] How this perspective challenges the Catholic Church in relation to its distinctive claims will be examined toward the end of the book.

---

10. This is in effect the teaching of John Paul II, *UUS* 28, on which see chapter 6.

5

Ecumenical Renewal

Embraced or Sidelined?

IT IS NOW NECESSARY to look at the history of CCR and its interaction with church authority to see to what extent this ecumenical grace has been acknowledged and received. This story is of relevance to all concerned with Christian unity and with the outpouring of the Holy Spirit in our day. For if the Lord's purpose is the renewal of the whole body of Christ as an essential element in the redemption of the human race and of all creation, then the reception of this ecumenical grace in the largest world communion can hardly be a matter of indifference to other Christians.

The First Phase (1967 to 1980)

The outbreak of the charismatic renewal released great hope and enthusiasm among those caught up in this move of the Holy Spirit. The excitement and joy was first the new experience of the Lord's love and presence, of entering into his praise, of knowing his loving attention to each believer. But the ecumenical dimension—enjoying a close heartfelt fellowship with other Christians—added to the excitement, and deepened the sense that something momentous was happening. In the first years of the renewal, most Catholics being baptized in the Spirit had little or no previous experience of fellowship with other Christians. The door to ecumenism for Catholics had only just been opened at Vatican Two. So for many the newness of their experience of the Lord went hand in hand with their experience of fellowship in the Spirit across church boundaries. As Catholics, they naturally interpreted this charismatic fellowship in ecumenical terms in line with the conciliar decree on ecumenism.

The major centers where the renewal first broke out in the USA were university campuses, among young Catholics often active in Catholic societies, and well aware of the new directions emerging from the Second Vatican Council. This was especially the case at the University of Michigan in Ann Arbor, at Michigan State University in Lansing, and at Notre Dame University in South Bend, Indiana. Many of the first participants were undergraduates or recent graduates, whose friendships and contacts spanned church boundaries, and who had been enthused by the council. In the postconciliar context, these young Catholics instinctively understood that this renewal in the Spirit was a grace for the renewal of the church. But their charismatic experience had an interdenominational dimension from the beginning. So the ecumenical dimension in the council and in the renewal helped them to understand it as a grace for the renewal of the whole body of Christ. Most had a focus on the renewal of the Catholic Church, within which ecumenical relations were an integral element. This vision of the renewal was expressed in an Ecumenical Statement issued by the Service Committee for the United States in 1973.[1]

When these young Catholics and young Protestants being baptized in the Spirit sensed the wonder of this interchurch fellowship, many sought to deepen and structure this new life by living in community. For them an ecumenical renewal led naturally to ecumenical community. In fact, they quickly pioneered new forms of community living that owed little to traditional forms of religious life. Among the original patterns were the formation of households for young singles, and the clustering of community families and households in housing developments, facilitating higher levels of interaction and sharing. In the Alleluia community in Augusta, Georgia, with majority Catholic but with a solid Episcopalian participation, the area of this clustering was named Faith Village, an identity that still exists forty years later. In these new interdenominational communities, the Catholics helped to imbue the Protestants with this ecumenical vision for the healing of Christian divisions.

The deep sense of sharing together the life in the Spirit led these North American communities to ground their mutual commitment in a

---

1. See Catholic, "Service Committee," 19–20.

covenantal relationship. Catholics and Protestants made covenant together. The front runner was the Word of God community, in Ann Arbor, whose membership at its peak in the late 1980s was approximately 65 percent Catholic and 35 percent Protestant.[2] This vision meant that the basic activities of each community as a whole were based on the common experience of new life through baptism in the Spirit, and on what was shared by all. At the same time they had no desire to detach themselves from their church traditions, but were committed to their renewal. So, typically, community members shared in their own church's worship on Sunday morning, and then took part in the community gatherings, often on Sunday afternoons or evenings. In the Word of God community, the need to provide church formation for children of community families led to the formation of four denominational fellowships (Catholic, Reformed, Lutheran, and Free Church), a model that was followed with variations in some other places.

This vision of ecumenical community did not generally commend itself to the Catholic authorities. The traditional pattern was that church loyalty was total, and so Catholics could never place themselves under the leadership of other Christians, even within an interdenominational community leadership with a Catholic majority. The conciliar constitution on the liturgy had formulated in a new way the centrality of the liturgy, and particularly the eucharist, for Catholic life: "the liturgy is the summit toward which the activity of the church is directed; it is also the source from which all its power flows."[3] The question arose: how could the liturgy be summit of the life of such an ecumenical community? So, while the Catholic Church had endorsed the movement for Christian unity, there were serious hesitations about the ecumenical covenant community model as a Catholic way forward.

However, the leaders of these communities were deeply convinced that it must be possible to base a community life on the God-given grace of baptism in the Spirit received alike by all. They believed that they were taking seriously the recognition of Pope John XXIII that what unites separated Christians is greater than what divides them. This is clearly one of the challenges to the churches posed by the whole charismatic movement, a point to which I will later return.

2. Other North American communities following this pattern included the People of Praise, South Bend, Indiana; the Work of Christ, Lansing, Michigan; the Servants of the Light, Minneapolis, Minnesota; Alleluia community, Augusta, Georgia; the Lamb of God in Baltimore, Maryland; and Mother of God, then in Potomac, Maryland. Unusually, the Work of Christ community had quite a number of Orthodox members.

3. *SC* 10.

This commitment to ecumenical community provided an ecumenical dynamism for the wider movement. These communities were largely composed of younger Christians under forty years of age (many leaders were under thirty at the time of their foundation), exhibiting a dynamism and commitment beyond what typically characterized the wider movement. The greater size and high level of commitment of the covenant communities produced greater resources of personnel and finances. As a result many dedicated young leaders were working full-time in charismatic service, and quickly came to dominate the newly-established structures for CCR, which in the first years were strongly supportive of an ecumenical vision.[4] This was especially true of the Word of God community, who produced *New Covenant Magazine*, and the People of Praise in South Bend, Indiana, who staffed Charismatic Renewal Services. The major communities played a key role in organizing the annual CCR conferences at Notre Dame, where the attendance multiplied rapidly in the early 1970s. Some Protestant speakers were always invited, and were warmly received. Some, like Pentecostal Vinson Synan, shared how they were won over from anti-Catholic prejudice to enthusiastic support.[5]

As the CCR structures developed between 1968 and 1972, the renewal movement within the Protestant churches was stimulated to develop their own denominational or confessional service organizations.[6] There was quickly some collaboration between Catholic and Lutheran charismatics. In the early 1970s, some Catholic leaders participated in the National Men's Charismatic Shepherds Conference, an initiative of some "nondenominational" leaders. The directors of the denominational agencies along with some "nondenominationals" formed an interdenominational committee, which became known as the Glencoe committee, that was soon planning the most successful interdenominational conference of all, held in Kansas City in July 1977, which we will discuss in more detail at the end of this section.

In Britain, the interchurch origins found expression primarily in Fountain Trust conferences and in local prayer groups. The Fountain Trust

4. For example, the National Service Committee in the United States, the National Communications Office, *New Covenant* magazine, the organization of major conferences for the general public and for leaders.

5. See Synan, *Bridges*.

6. The only group already existing was the Charismatic Communion of Presbyterian Ministers, formed in 1966 to defend charismatic ministers accused of heresy or other deviations. In the 1970s, this became the Presbyterian Charismatic Communion, aiming like its parallel organizations to spread renewal in its confessional family.

was founded by Anglican priest Michael Harper in 1964, and did much through conferences and literature to make the charismatic movement known among Protestant Christians. Its ethos tended to have an Anglican flavor, but Harper involved leaders from the nondenominational sector as well as the older free churches. As soon as he read the first book on the outbreak among Catholics, Harper invited its authors, Kevin and Dorothy Ranaghan, to a Fountain Trust conference in Guildford held in the summer of 1971. In Dublin, Ireland, Cardinal Suenens shared the platform in 1975 with Tom Smail, Michael Harper's successor at the Fountain Trust. The cardinal, who had developed a good relationship with Smail, a very capable theologian, accepted invitations to speak at the Fountain Trust conferences in Westminster, London, in 1977 and 1979.[7] Such initiatives generated great hopes, and were seen as breakthrough events. In the conflict situation of Northern Ireland, the only popular conference for many years to gather Protestants and Catholics was charismatic.

With their greater resources and a high level of commitment, the Word of God community from Ann Arbor soon developed an extensive international outreach. Ecumenical communities grew up in West London, England; in Belfast, Northern Ireland; and in Beirut, Lebanon. In 1975, an association of communities was formed which also included Emmanuel community in Brisbane, Australia. However, this association came to an end within four years largely because of differences in vision and methods between Word of God in Ann Arbor and the People of Praise in South Bend.

In France, the years from 1972 to 1974 saw a flowering of new charismatic communities, whose ethos and ecclesio-cultural sensitivities were noticeably different from the North American covenant communities.[8] Of the major French communities, only Chemin Neuf had an ecumenical vision, describing themselves as a "Catholic community with an ecumenical calling."[9] This vision led to their having Protestant members, a few in leadership roles. In French-speaking Europe, the strongest ecumenical impulse came from Thomas Roberts, who had gone to France in the 1920s as a missionary of the Apostolic Church, and who always retained his

7. See Au, *Grassroots Unity*.

8. The major communities in the first twenty-five years were Emmanuel community, Chemin Neuf, Béatitudes (originally called the Lion of Judah), and Pain de Vie.

9. A less-known French community with an ecumenical vision and membership is Puits de Jacob near Strasbourg, founded by Fr. Bertrand Lepesant, SJ (see chapter 1).

Pentecostal fire and convictions. The decision to remain in France during the German occupation won him a place in French hearts, and enabled him to play a national role when the charismatic renewal arrived. Roberts was loved and revered as a man of unity and reconciliation throughout the French-speaking world, even among those in CCR not so open to ecumenical expressions. Roberts belonged to the Union de Prière of Charmes-sur-Rhône, a nonresidential French Reformed community, founded after the second World War in the wake of a charismatic revival in the Ardèche in the 1930s. Their members were excited by the news of the charismatic movement, and helped to make possible a remarkable meeting held at Viviers in the autumn of 1973, that truly demonstrated the ecumenical potential of the nascent movement. Besides David du Plessis, Anglican leader Michael Harper from England, and Lutheran Arnold Bittlinger from Germany, many priests and pastors gathered, the majority not participants in the renewal, but interested to learn more.[10] Pastor Georges Appia, a senior reformed pastor, wrote: "We found ourselves in the presence of a living manifestation of Christian unity, of which we have had few examples, even in the most favorable situations. Whether in study, prayer, praise, or reflection in working groups, there was a surprising transparency and unanimity between all the participants. But at the same time there was a clear resolve not to do anything that could involve any scandal for the members of our communities or a break with church authority."[11]

In West Germany, an ecumenical charismatic community was established in 1968 at Schloss Craheim, which had Lutheran, Catholic, and Baptist members. Among the Lutherans was Pastor Arnold Bittlinger, who was the author of two short biblical treatises for charismatic Christians.[12] For a few years, Schloss Craheim acted as a center of inspiration for the renewal in Germany. The first meeting of the European Charismatic Leaders Conference took place there in 1972, the first interdenominational charismatic body to be formed.

The apex of the first stage of charismatic enthusiasm for Christian unity came with the North American conference that drew over fifty thousand participants to Kansas City, Missouri, in July 1977. Organized

10. More than sixty pastors took part at Viviers. Most were from the French Reformed Church, fifteen from Switzerland, representatives of Protestant communities of sisters, and some forty priests, including Jesuits, Dominicans, Benedictines, and Trappists, together with those from the new communities.

11. Viviers, 4 (author's translation).

12. Bittlinger, *Gifts and Graces*, and *Gifts and Ministries*.

by the Glencoe committee of leaders from the various renewal organizations, the Kansas City gathering pioneered a new form of ecumenical
structuring. In the mornings, each church/confessional family or stream
held its own session with worship and teaching. The Catholic contingent
was the largest of these with twenty-five thousand, with the second in
numbers being one of the nondenominational groupings.[13] In the afternoons, there were workshops given by teachers from all backgrounds,
with participants being free to go wherever they chose. In the evenings,
there was a mass gathering of all participants in the Arrowhead stadium,
which provided the most memorable moments of the conference. These
included powerful messages concerning unity from the major leaders,
significant prophetic words, and the sight of Cardinal Suenens from Belgium sitting alongside Thomas Zimmerman, the general superintendent
of the North American Assemblies of God.

Urged by former staff member Walter Hollenweger, the World Council of Churches began to take notice of the charismatic phenomenon, and
organized a consultation on the significance of the charismatic renewal for
the churches at Bossey, Switzerland, in 1980, which was attended by several scholars from the renewal.[14] The consultation had been preceded by a
questionnaire sent to all member churches of the WCC, which elicited a
quantity of documentation often indicating that church officials were not
well informed on the subject.[15]

Ecclesial Integration or Denominational Retrenchment? (1980 to 1995)

By 1980, the extraordinary growth of CCR in North America seemed to
have peaked. By this time, the renewal had spread throughout the world,
even reaching a few nations where Christianity was persecuted and severely
repressed. As it spread to predominantly Catholic countries, there was less

---

13. Because of the dispute among nondenominationals over discipling and shep-
herding, there were two nondenominational streams that met separately. The larger was
the discipling-shepherding group led by the Christian Growth Ministries team from Fort
Lauderdale, Florida.

14. Heribert Mühlen, Kilian McDonnell, OSB, and the present author were among
the Catholics present.

15. The papers presented at Bossey were published in Bittlinger, *Church*.

awareness of its ecumenical origins, despite the fact that even in such places Protestants had sometimes played a role in its arrival.[16]

Among Catholics, there was a strong desire that the renewal be received and welcomed into the full life of the Catholic Church. A distinctive feature of the Catholic beginnings was that leaders saw clearly that this renewal was for the whole church. The warm welcome of Paul VI at the international conference in Rome in 1975 came with astonishing rapidity only eight years after the beginnings at the Duquesne weekend. In fact, this recognition came without any playing down of the ecumenical dimension.[17] By the early 1980s, CCR leaders were talking about the renewal "moving to the heart of the church," a slogan accompanying the move of the international office from Brussels to Rome in 1981. The desire that the grace of the renewal should permeate all dimensions of Catholic life (liturgical, catechetical, pastoral, and missionary) at all levels (international, national, diocesan, and parochial) was clearly right. But perhaps inevitably, this process led to a playing down of the ecumenical dimension, as renewal often now meant simply Catholic renewal without reference to charismatic renewal in other churches and ecclesial communities. This Catholic-centered thinking was necessary in dealing with the Vatican, where everything concerning other Christians was the concern of the Vatican body for ecumenical relations,[18] while all Catholic renewal came under the responsibility of different Roman congregations and councils (doctrine, worship, clergy, education, laity, etc.).[19] Organizationally, to insist on the ecumenical dimension as intrinsic to renewal introduced a confusing factor. But few people asked what kind of renewal is moving to the heart of the church. Was it the renewal with its full ecumenical and prophetic potential, or was it a somewhat "sanitized" version that was indubitably orthodox, but less challenging than the renewal as it came from the hand of the Lord?

In some of the countries where Catholic Charismatic Renewal had its greatest initial impact (USA, Ireland, Quebec), the movement began

16. For example, in Colombia, Peru, Ecuador.

17. See Suenens, *New Pentecost?*

18. At that time, still known as the Secretariat for Promoting Christian Unity, but later renamed the Pontifical Council for the Promotion of the Unity of Christians.

19. By the late 1980s, CCR as a "new ecclesial movement" became a particular responsibility of the Pontifical Council for the Laity. There was a period when Bishop Paul Cordes, secretary at the Council for the Laity, had a particular personal responsibility for CCR as successor to Cardinal Suenens, as well as his role in relation to all the new movements.

to decline in the 1980s. Not a few observers have noted a connection between a pulling back from the ecumenical dimension and the decline of
the renewal. The marginalizing of the ecumenical dimension reduces the
prophetic challenges of the renewal, weakens its biblical grounding, and
can tend to relegate it to the sphere of piety. In the immediate aftermath
of the council and the emphasis on liturgical renewal, the old-style Catholic devotions had often declined. With the growth of charismatic prayer
groups, there was often a dearth of solid teaching, and the resultant void
easily led to meetings becoming more devotional. By the second half of the
1980s, the popularity of prayer groups based on the Marian apparitions in
Medjugorje in Herzegovina-Bosnia meant that in some places, notably in
Ireland, charismatic groups frequently morphed into Medjugorje groups.

The Catholic difficulties concerning interdenominational expressions
of renewal reached their peak at the end of the 1980s. Immediately following a gathering of the newly-formed European Charismatic Consultation
at Disentis, Switzerland, in June 1989, the Catholics present stayed on for a
day, and agreed on a statement concerning the renewal and Christian unity.[20] This statement, signed by all the Catholics present, emphasized the essentially ecumenical character of the charismatic movement.[21] However, an
address of Bishop Paul Cordes, officially responsible for CCR, to a leaders
conference in October of that year effectively prevented this statement from
being used within CCR. This episode occurred in the midst of the Vatican's
efforts to consolidate CCR within the Catholic Church, a policy intended to
encourage Catholic charismatic communities dealing with often-unsympa-
thetic bishops. In this climate there was a danger that Catholics would not
be allowed to take part in the interdenominational conferences at Bern in
1990 (European), or at Brighton in 1991 (worldwide). Among those who
helped to reassure Bishop Cordes at that time were Kim Kollins, Fr. Raniero
Cantalamessa, and Charles Whitehead. In the end there was a full Catholic
participation and presence at Brighton, which showed again the astonishing breadth in the overall Pentecostal-charismatic spectrum. Brighton was
also notable for including a theological track.[22]

20. This statement was published in *Good News,* the newsletter of CCR in England
and Wales, Nov–Dec 1989.

21. See Appendix for the text. One of the signatories was Fr. Paul Lebeau, SJ who had
been the personal theological adviser to Cardinal Suenens.

22. Some papers from the theological track were published in Hunter and Hocken,
All Together.

Difficulties in the Ecumenical Communities

Another factor discouraging ecumenical expressions of charismatic renewal were the difficulties encountered by most of the ecumenical communities. From the 1970s, there had been tensions between the communities and the rest of the renewal. These tensions existed in several countries, but were strongest in the United States, with complaints that the communities dominated the service committee, the publications, and the conferences with their distinctive style and emphases. As a result there were brief and not very successful attempts to launch alternatives, inevitably less ecumenical, such as the magazine *Catholic Charismatic*, and a different set of Life in the Spirit seminars. The diocesan liaisons for the renewal, appointed by the bishops, who were mostly priests, formed their own organization, which served as a counterbalance to the national service committee.

In France, which also had fast-expanding charismatic communities, the concentration of power in the communities was reduced by their unique national renewal structure, called *L'Instance nationale*, which is a commission of the Episcopal conference attended by representatives from the communities and the prayer groups. Yet even here the leaders of the Catholic charismatic prayer groups felt the need to organize a major national event for their followers independently of the communities, with many being surprised that twenty thousand came to this festival at Le Bourget near Paris in 1988.[23]

These difficulties were most clearly manifested in some splits and crises that particularly affected the North American communities. The most serious was the division in the Word of God community at Ann Arbor around 1989 to 1990. In consequence, the charismatic communities in the United States no longer exercised a significant influence on the movement, which by this time had decreased in numbers and intensity. But the wane of community influence meant a lesser attention to the ecumenical dimension.

Unity Dimension Never Forgotten

Although the ecumenical dimension of the renewal never became a major focus, and some Catholics played it down in the interests of full church

23. This gathering led to the formation of an association for Catholic charismatic prayer groups, known as *Pentecôte*.

acceptance, it never disappeared. The massive interdenominational conference held at Kansas City in July 1977, was both a high point in the initial growth of the renewal, and of its ecumenical expression. In Europe the high point was the remarkable conference "Pentecost over Europe," held in Strasbourg in 1982, which was the brainchild of Thomas Roberts. Attracting twenty thousand participants from many European countries, Strasbourg 1982 provided a strong ecumenical élan and inspiration.

However, the charismatic movement constantly throws up new trends, new emphases, and new patterns. In the midst of this creativity, the pioneers were being reminded of the earlier ecumenical fire, while new ecumenical impulses were arising, sometimes from unexpected sources. Three men played a major role internationally: Michael Harper (Anglican), Larry Christenson (Lutheran), and Fr. Tom Forrest (Catholic), who first came together in 1983. After consultations in Singapore (1987, 1988), and a prayer vigil in Jerusalem (1993), an executive committee for a new body was formed with two Protestants, two Catholics, and two Pentecostals.[24] This worldwide interdenominational charismatic body was initially called the International Charismatic Consultation on World Evangelization (IC-COWE), and demonstrated its potential at the Brighton conference in 1991. Around the same time continental interchurch bodies were formed: North American Renewal Services Committee (NARSC), and the European Charismatic Consultation (ECC).

Indicative of the Holy Spirit's raising up of new initiatives was the friendship in southern Italy between Matteo Calisi, a Catholic charismatic leader from Bari, and Giovanni Traettino, a Pentecostal pastor from Caserta. Their partnership led to a series of annual conferences in Italy on Catholics and Evangelicals in dialogue, with international ecumenical speakers, and later to Calisi and Traettino witnessing together to reconciliation in other nations.

A More Nuanced Evaluation

It is possible to reach the conclusion that the extraordinary ecumenical potential of the charismatic renewal manifest in its origins and opening phase was largely wasted. Perhaps the main evidence supporting such a view would be the minimal interaction over these years before 1995 between the

24. The nondenominationals were bracketed with the Pentecostals. The two Catholics chosen were Fr. Tom Forrest and Kim Kollins.

charismatic movement and the ecumenical movement. This is rather ex-traordinary, since these two movements are major distinguishing features of twentieth-century Christianity. But it is also clear that the ecumenical impulses in the renewal have never disappeared, and they keep resurfac-ing. Nonetheless, it would seem that the second and third generation of renewal leaders for the most part do not manifest the same ecumenical zeal as the pioneers of the first generation. But there are notable exceptions, such as Charles Whitehead (England), Matteo Calisi (Italy), and Johannes Fichtenbauer (Austria).[25]

However, as the years have passed, I have come to a more nuanced evaluation. With hindsight, I see that in the first years of the Catholic Char-ismatic Renewal the time was not ripe for the development of a charismatic ecumenism. A major reason was the very recent conversion of the Catho-lic Church to an ecumenical vision. Remarkably, the vast majority of the bishops who voted to approve the decree on ecumenism in 1964 had no ecumenical experience whatever. The decree was so good because of the dedicated work over many often difficult years of highly committed and talented ecumenical pioneers.[26]

Understandably and rightly, the initial ecumenical initiatives taken by the Catholic Church were concerned with developing positive relations, and a better mutual understanding between different ecclesial groupings and traditions. The strongest focus was on theological dialogue, with Cath-olic participants being chosen for their professional competence and their deep grounding in the Catholic tradition. In general, lay Catholics becom-ing ecumenically involved were well-educated and intellectually coherent. While some Catholics baptized in the Spirit had received some theological formation, the vast majority had not; the movement was not galvanized by theology, but the shared experience of baptism in the Spirit. These factors made the profiles of the charismatic and the ecumenical movements very different from each other, and help to explain the lack of interaction over many years between these two movements initiated by the Holy Spirit.

25. Fr. Laurent Fabre, the founder and shepherd of the Chemin Neuf community, now found in many nations, remains one of the early leaders continuing to preach a strongly ecumenical message.

26. Among these should be mentioned the Abbé Paul Couturier from France, and Dom Lambert Beauduin from Belgium, who had both died before the decree was writ-ten, and others who participated such as Père Yves Congar, OP (France); Msgr. Jan Wil-lebrands (Netherlands); Père Jean Corbon (Lebanon); Père Pierre Duprey; and Fr. Tom Stransky (USA).

Further, the charismatic movement was too amorphous to fit into the emerging ecumenical patterns. While the charismatic Catholics understood their charismatic experience with other Christians within the framework of the ecumenism newly approved by the council, and some Protestant charismatics—especially the Lutherans—understood it in a similar way, the majority of charismatic Protestants in the 1970s lacked a vision for church renewal and were weakly organized.[27] Moreover, the overall movement included "nondenominational" elements, many of which did not believe that renewal of the older churches was possible, and in its more zealous expressions advocated a "come out and join us" policy. As a consequence, the first two Catholic books on the renewal and ecumenism both devoted much effort to distinguishing between an approach that is "ecumenical," and one that is "nondenominational."[28] A charismatic ecumenism spreading like wildfire among enthusiastic laity did not fit into the newly developing framework of Catholic ecumenism. This helps to explain, for example, why there is not a single reference to the renewal or to charismatic prayer groups in the Ecumenical Directory published by the Vatican in 1993.

Undoubtedly ecumenists could have done more to recognize the ecumenical potential of the renewal, and renewal leaders could have done more to serve the wider ecumenical cause. But in retrospect and in the light of new developments since 1995,[29] we can more readily understand that the time was not ripe for a charismatic ecumenism in the 1970s and the 1980s. Nonetheless, over these years the Holy Spirit kept alive the flame for Christian unity in preparation for a more propitious hour to strike.

27. This situation was not improved in the 1980s with a major influx into the charismatic sphere of Evangelicals for whom connecting with the church of history was not among their priorities.

28. Suenens, *Ecumenism*; McDonnell, *Renewal and Ecumenism*.

29. See chapter 6.

II

Toward a Charismatic Contribution to Ecumenism

6

A New Season

WHILE THE ECUMENICAL DIMENSION in the origins of the charismatic movement did not produce the breakthrough for Christian unity that many expected in the early days of the renewal, the ecumenical bonds formed by the common experience of baptism in the Spirit were never entirely forgotten. New ecumenical initiatives continued to spring up, often in unexpected places. However, the overall climate began to warm up around the year 1995. There are signs that the hour is now ripe for a significant charismatic contribution to ecumenism in a way for which the renewal and the churches were not ready thirty years earlier.

New Thinking in Ecumenical Circles

By the mid-1990s an increasing number of Christians committed to Christian unity were concerned about the diminishing credibility of the ecumenical movement, and its lack of appeal to the younger generation. There was a widespread feeling that ecumenism had "run out of gas," and lacked the dynamic vision necessary to attract the younger generation. The official movement often gave the impression of being as bureaucratic as the denominations it hoped to inspire and renew. The decreasing credibility came above all from the combination of two factors: firstly, from the fast-growing segment of Evangelical, Pentecostal, and charismatic Christians, most of whom regarded official ecumenism as dead religion or apostate Christianity; secondly, from the decreasing membership and influence of the ecumenical churches in

Europe and North America, who provide most of the finances. As a result the percentage of Christians belonging to churches and denominations forming part of the World Council of Churches was steadily decreasing.

In this situation, some WCC officials in Geneva became convinced that a new initiative was needed to bring together Christians from every type of tradition, movement, and background. In particular, they thought it necessary to reach out to those Evangelicals and Pentecostals who did not want anything to do with the existing ecumenical structures. Ten years of assiduous building of bridges and holding of regional consultations led to the birth in 2007 of the Global Christian Forum (GCF), bringing together Christian leaders from all traditions and streams, and organized in a way to ensure that at least half the participation would be from Evangelical and Pentecostal churches.[1] A totally new approach was adopted for the first Global Assembly of GCF in Limuru, Kenya, in 2007. No titles were to be used. The delegates were divided into groups of approximately twenty people, and they began with each person sharing who Jesus Christ is for them. Pentecostal scholars Wonsuk Ma (Korea) and Cheryl Bridges Johns (USA) gave the two major addresses. The Limuru meeting opened up new channels of communication, and there was virtually unanimous agreement that the process should continue. It is too early to say what the long-term implications will be, and what direction GCF might take, but clearly in some way an ecumenical logjam has been broken.[2]

Since the Limuru meeting, together with the ecumenists from the Catholic Church, a representative of CCR has been invited to join (Charles Whitehead from England) and at the second Global Assembly of GCF in October 2011, held in Manado, Indonesia, Michelle Moran from International Catholic Charismatic Renewal Services was a keynote speaker. These are signs of recognition of the ecumenical importance of the renewal movement.

Major Developments in the Pentecostal and Charismatic Worlds

Pentecostal Theology

A significant development with major ecumenical potential is the emergence in the worldwide Pentecostal movement of serious scholarship

---

1. See Van Beek, *Revisioning*.
2. GCF has now appointed a full-time general secretary, Larry Miller, a Mennonite.

(theological, exegetical, and historical) that is interacting with scholars from other Christian traditions. As a result, the deep suspicion of ecumenism among Pentecostals, seeing it as a merely human effort to counteract inevitable decline, is giving way to more open attitudes, and among some to a real ecumenical commitment. At present, this tendency is found in academic and educational circles more strongly than in denominational leadership. It is most advanced in North America, where the Society for Pentecostal Studies now has an ecumenical interest group that is fully accepted as part of the Society, but more open attitudes are also developing in Asia and in Latin America, and not only among the scholars.

Another consequence of the rise of significant Pentecostal scholarship is the emergence of theological writing on themes that equally concern the charismatic renewal, such as baptism in the Spirit. Pentecostals are more motivated to reflect on baptism in the Spirit, since this is at the heart of their Christian and denominational life. Pentecostal Frank Macchia's study *Baptized in the Spirit* leaves behind the narrowly intra-Pentecostal debates, and presents a creative vision of a Spirit-baptized church.[3] In this way, Macchia provides an approach that can greatly enrich the understanding of baptism in the Spirit for all charismatic Christians.[4]

The New Charismatic Churches

In the last thirty years, there has been a veritable explosion of new charismatic-type assemblies and networks all over the world. Many of these, especially in Europe and North America, began with a rude dismissal of the relevance of the historic churches. But unlike some sectarian movements, their thinking was not primarily doctrinal or theological (we don't associate with you because your beliefs are wrong), but much more pragmatic (we don't have time for you because your churches have no life). But by the 1990s and a second generation of "nondenominationalism," this haughty attitude was dissolving, largely through new church charismatics recognizing the work of the Spirit in historic church renewal circles. The first changes here were much helped by March for Jesus, an initiative of the new charismatic groups, but have been carried further by the Alpha course, an

3. Macchia, *Baptized*.

4. A subsequent book by Macchia, *Justified*, shows how a Pentecostal understanding of the central role of the Holy Spirit can deepen and aid the Catholic-Lutheran debate on justification by faith.

Anglican initiative for evangelism taken up with enthusiasm by many of the "new charismatics." Such cooperation would have been unimaginable twenty years earlier.[5]

In the late 1990s discussions began to take place about a possible initiative involving new church charismatic leaders with leaders from CCR. A prime mover was Kim Kollins, an American convert to Catholicism from an independent charismatic background, who had come to Europe as a missionary, and rather quickly became a Catholic.[6] The fruit has been a series of meetings entitled Gatherings in the Holy Spirit, gathering leaders from both sides and meeting every two years—always in Rome at the request of the "nondenominationals."[7] From these meetings came provisional discussions between the "nondenom" leaders and officials of the Pontifical Council for Promoting the Unity of Christians, which have led in 2012 to the decision to begin a three-year round of conversations in 2014 on the theme, "Authority, Revelation, and the Word of God."

Official Pentecostal Attitudes

Although most Pentecostal denominations have remained outside the organized ecumenical structures, their attitudes towards ecumenical relations have nonetheless been changing. From an outright opposition to all ecumenism, many Pentecostal bodies have moved to a stance of hesitation and even qualified sympathy. This is shown by their welcome of the GCF initiative, free from all institutional implications. One element in this change is surely the advance in theological skills already noted. Another sign is the report on Evangelization, Proselytism, and Common Witness from the Roman Catholic-Pentecostal dialogue issued in 1997. For the first time, there was a balanced bilateral statement on the sensitive issue of Pentecostal evangelism among Catholic populations. This report no doubt helped to prepare the ground for the more recent joint document, "Christian Witness in a Multi-Religious World: Recommendations for Conduct," issued in 2011 from the WCC, the World Evangelical Alliance, and the Pontifical Council for Inter-religious Dialogue. There is a recognition in these documents of the right to proclaim the gospel message without pressure, that

5. See section on the Alpha Course at the end of this chapter.

6. See Kollins, *It's only*.

7. The Catholic participants are all leaders in CCR, with the exception of Fr. James Puglisi, SA and Teresa Francesca Rossi from the Centro pro Unione in Rome.

allays some Pentecostal fears about ecumenism undermining evangelism, a recognition that helps Pentecostal leaders to recognize positive fruits from interchurch discussions.

It is also significant that when the Pentecostal movement celebrated its centenary in 2006, a Catholic charismatic leader was invited to become a member of the Centennial Planning Committee. Charles Whitehead played this role with the approval of Cardinal Kasper, then president of the Pontifical Council for Promoting the Unity of Christians.

The Contribution of John Paul II

For Catholics it is easy to recognize 1995 as a key moment, being the year of issue of John Paul II's encyclical letter on ecumenism, *Ut Unum Sint*. This may be the only papal encyclical that begins with a personal declaration: "I carry out this duty with the profound conviction that I am obeying the Lord, and with a clear sense of my own human frailty."[8]

Although *Ut Unum Sint* nowhere mentions the charismatic movement, the emphases of the encyclical rejoiced the heart of charismatic Catholics. A central feature is its strong reaffirmation of the *spiritual ecumenism* of the decree on ecumenism. In para. 15 the Pope underlines the link between ecumenism and conversion, and in para. 16 he insists on "a clear connection between renewal, conversion, and reform." Here the pope is taking up and developing the teaching of Vatican Two in paras. 6–8 of the decree on ecumenism. Although he does not mention the Abbé Paul Couturier, the French pioneer of "spiritual ecumenism" (and originator of this phrase), John Paul II was clearly seeing these paragraphs as the motor of ecumenical advance.[9]

The pope does not comment directly on the developments in the ecumenical movement in the thirty years between Vatican Two and 1995. But his encyclical can be read as a strong corrective, summoning the movement back to its spiritual foundations and core principles. After Vatican Two, the Catholic Church initiated many bilateral theological dialogues with other world communions. At the same time, Catholics officially entered into many ecumenical activities through Councils of Churches, Churches

8. *UUS* 4.

9. Pope Benedict XVI referred to Couturier as "the father of spiritual ecumenism" in an "Ecumenical Meeting" address at the World Youth Day in Cologne, Germany, in 2005. (See website link in bibliography.)

Together, and other interchurch agencies. There was a multiplication of ecumenical structures, but in this process spiritual ecumenism tended to recede into the background, sometimes being reduced to annual observance of the Week of Prayer for Christian Unity.

One of the longest sections in the encyclical is entitled "The Primacy of Prayer."[10] This goes further than Vatican Two, which was much more cautious, since at that time Catholics had minimal experience of common prayer with other Christians.[11] But in *UUS*, there is a boldness, a confidence in the Holy Spirit, that was a hallmark of John Paul II. "Love is the great undercurrent which gives life and adds vigor to the movement towards unity. This love finds its most complete expression in common prayer."[12] In fact the pope is quite lyrical about the experience of common prayer: "Along the ecumenical path to unity, pride of place certainly belongs to common prayer, the prayerful union of those who gather together around Christ himself. If Christians, despite their divisions, can grow ever more united in common prayer around Christ, they will grow in the awareness of how little divides them in comparison to what unites them."[13] That this is not recommending a cozy huddle is clear from what follows: "If they meet more often and more regularly before Christ in prayer, they will be able to gain the courage to face all the painful human reality of their divisions, and they will find themselves together once more in that community of the church which Christ constantly builds up in the Holy Spirit, in spite of all weaknesses and human limitations."[14]

Though there is no mention of the renewal, these sections really resonate with all who have been baptized in the Spirit. For the renewal introduced prayer with other Christians to Catholic experience at the grassroots level on a massive scale. "Prayer, the community at prayer, enables us always to discover anew the evangelical truth of the words: 'You have one Father' (Matt 23:9), the Father—Abba . . . Ecumenical prayer discloses this fundamental dimension of brotherhood in Christ."[15] Because the renewal has been grounded in a common experience of the Holy Spirit, an inner

10. *UUS* 21–27.

11. "In certain special circumstances . . . it is allowable, indeed desirable that Catholics should join in prayer with their separated brethren." *UR* 8.

12. *UUS* 21.

13. Ibid., 22.

14. Ibid.

15. Ibid., 26.

conviction is produced that what unites is more fundamental than what divides, which for many others has remained a theory that has not been felt at heart level.

For John Paul II, as for the Abbé Couturier, all ecumenism requires a spiritual dimension. Spiritual ecumenism cannot be reduced to one branch of work for unity, alongside but separate from other branches such as theological ecumenism and practical collaborative ecumenism. This is clear from the emphasis on mutual repentance for sins against unity: "In a corresponding way, there is an increased sense of the need for repentance: an awareness of certain exclusions which seriously harm fraternal charity, of certain refusals to forgive, of a certain pride, of an unevangelical insistence on condemning the 'other side,' of a disdain born of an unhealthy presumption."[16]

The teaching of the encyclical on ecumenical dialogue makes clear the spiritual character of all dialogue between separated Christians. Here again John Paul II is able to go deeper into the character of ecumenical encounter: "Dialogue is not simply an exchange of ideas. In some way it is always an 'exchange of gifts.'"[17] Each Christian tradition is the bearer of gifts—for the whole body. This insight is the fruit of the christological transformation that was at the heart of Couturier's contribution: effecting a shift from church-centered relations to an ecclesial Christ-centeredness. Instead of the pre-ecumenical approach that started from what is wrong with the doctrine of the others, one asks first: what are the gifts of the other? One is in effect asking: what is the work of the Holy Spirit in this tradition? This paradigm shift fits with the experience of renewal as receiving all the gifts from the Lord that he has through us through opening ourselves to the Holy Spirit.

In paragraphs 33–35 the pope speaks of ecumenical dialogue as an examination of conscience. This is a visionary ideal, and was not a description of ecumenism as typically practiced from 1965 to 1995. The pope speaks of dialogue as involving three partners, not just two church communities, but of two church communities meeting in the presence of the Lord, and being in dialogue also with him. This insight demonstrates clearly the spiritual dimension in theological dialogue. It leads right into a deep spiritual recognition about humble confession of sin:

16. Ibid., 15.
17. Ibid., 28.

Dialogue cannot take place merely on a horizontal level, being restricted to meetings, exchanges of points of view, or even the sharing of gifts proper to each community. It has also a primarily vertical thrust, directed towards the One who, as the redeemer of the world and the Lord of history, is himself our reconciliation. This vertical aspect of dialogue lies in our acknowledgment, jointly and to each other, that we are men and women who have sinned. It is precisely this [acknowledgment] which creates in brothers and sisters living in communities not in full communion with one another that interior space where Christ, the source of the church's unity, can effectively act, with all the power of his Spirit, [the Paraclete].[18]

Another original contribution of John Paul II to ecumenism lies in his reflections on the importance of martyrs for Christian unity.[19] He introduces this theme by referring back to para. 34 about "the spiritual space in which each community hears the call to overcome the obstacles to unity. . . . All of them in fact have martyrs for the Christian faith. . . . In a theocentric vision, we Christians already have a common martyrology."[20] Why is this? Our "communion is already perfect in what we all consider the highest point of the life of grace, martyria unto death, the truest communion possible with Christ who shed his Blood."[21]

Finally, the pope addressed his own role and responsibility in relation to Christian unity, seeing the bishop of Rome as "the first servant of unity."[22] "As bishop of Rome I am fully aware, as I have reaffirmed in the present Encyclical Letter, that Christ ardently desires the full and visible communion of all those Communities in which, by virtue of God's faithfulness, his Spirit dwells. I am convinced that I have a particular responsibility in this regard, above all in acknowledging the ecumenical aspirations of the majority of the Christian Communities."[23] John Paul II then gave an unexpected invitation. He asked leaders and theologians of other churches to join him in seeking out a new way of exercising the

18. Ibid., 34.

19. John Paul II, who had personally known martyrs for the faith under Nazi and Communist persecution, had already introduced a theology of martyrdom into an earlier encyclical letter, *Veritatis Splendor* on moral teaching (1993).

20. *UUS* 83–84.

21. Ibid., 84.

22. Ibid., 94.

23. Ibid., 95.

papal ministry that would truly serve the cause of unity while remaining faithful to its essential mission.[24]

In the conclusion to the encyclical, the pope asked three times: How is the church to obtain this grace of full unity? First answer, through prayer. Second answer, through giving thanks. Third answer, through hope in the Spirit.[25]

Although *Ut Unum Sint* does not mention the renewal, its reemphasis of spiritual ecumenism provides an essential foundation for all charismatic contributions to Christian unity. Its reaffirmation that what unites is deeper and more important than what divides provides the basis for taking seriously the shared experience of charismatic Christians from different traditions. Its presentation of dialogue as an exchange of gifts is illustrated by the experience of the charismatic renewal, in which there has been a greater sharing in the Spirit than has been general between the churches. Its insistence that dialogue involves an examination of conscience highlights the role of the Holy Spirit, for only the Holy Spirit can convict of sin (see John 16:8–11).

In the wake of *Ut Unum Sint*, there is evidence that the Pontifical Council for Promoting Christian Unity is attributing a higher importance to what its president, Cardinal Walter Kasper, described in 2007 as "a third wave of Christian history: the diffusion of charismatic and Pentecostal groups who, with about four hundred million faithful throughout the world, take second place among the Christian communities in numerical terms and are experiencing exponential growth."[26]

The Alpha Course

Also in the mid-1990s another development of major ecumenical significance arose from Evangelical and charismatic roots. The Alpha course, developed especially by Rev. Nicky Gumbel at Holy Trinity Anglican parish in Brompton, London, began to be promoted beyond its parish of origin. Alpha is "low-key charismatic." While it has a Holy Spirit weekend and refers openly to the possibility of receiving the gift of tongues, it presents the basic gospel without using charismatic terminology. The Alpha

24. See *UUS* 96.

25. Ibid., 102.

26. Kasper, "Address," 187. Cardinal Kasper's successor, Cardinal Kurt Koch, recently urged the need to pay more attention to this "fourth form of Christianity."

course quickly reached a wide range of local congregations, Anglican and older free church, as well as new charismatic churches, first in Britain and quickly elsewhere.

Although Alpha was slow to win acceptance among Catholics in its first phase of expansion from 1994, Gumbel has devoted intensifying efforts to reach the Catholic world in the last fifteen years. The result is that in 2013, the Alpha course is growing fastest among Catholics with an amazingly strong following among Latin Americans. The Catholic welcome has intensified since Pope Benedict XVI's call for a New Evangelization, with Alpha being welcomed by several Vatican officials and many bishops, (but not so many in Europe!), as a vital tool for the New Evangelization. Nicky Gumbel was received enthusiastically at the International Eucharistic Congress in Dublin in June 2012.

The extraordinary impact of the Alpha course across all churches and continents has quietly been creating a situation in which millions of Christians have received the same pattern of evangelism and awakening of faith. It is too soon to measure the long-term effects, but this remarkable expansion surely has to facilitate in a significant way the collaboration and coming together of the churches.

Other Signs

The signs that the time is approaching when the charismatic contribution to Christian unity can be welcomed are confirmed by recent developments in the Catholic Fraternity of Charismatic Covenant Communities and Fellowships. When the Fraternity was founded in the early 1990s with strong Vatican encouragement, it reflected both the official desire to have strong Catholic communities, and the concern that any ecumenical dimension would endanger this goal. However, in 2002 the Catholic Fraternity elected Matteo Calisi from Bari, Italy, the founder and leader of the Comunità di Gesù in Bari, Italy, a strong proponent of charismatic ecumenism, as their president.[27] Slowly, the ethos of the fraternity has moved away from the thinking that being ecumenical means being less Catholic, so that in April 2012, the fraternity chose ecumenism and the new evangelization as the

27. Matteo Calisi has promoted regular celebrations in Bari, bringing together church leaders from an astonishing spectrum of Christian churches and movements, some addressing justice and peace issues, some on worship, some on messianic Judaism.

theme for its Assisi gatherings.[28] Differently from twenty-five years earlier, there was no nervousness being expressed about recognizing the ecumenical character of the renewal either from the participants, or from invited speakers including those from the Vatican. It is clear that the atmosphere today is much more propitious to the development of an ecumenism of renewal that is fully respectful of ecclesial commitments and convictions.

Matteo Calisi has also taken a strong interest in developing positive relations with Pentecostals and nondenominational charismatics. With the help of a daughter community in Buenos Aires, he developed contacts in Argentina with local Evangelical and Pentecostal leaders, with whom a new body was formed; the movement known as CRECES (literally, Renewed or Restored Communion of Catholics and Evangelicals in the Holy Spirit).[29] From the beginning, Catholic archbishop of Buenos Aires, Cardinal Jorge Mario Bergoglio, SJ, now Pope Francis, supported CRECES. Cardinal Bergoglio played a regular part in CRECES gatherings, and was prayed over by leading Pentecostal pastors, together with Fr. Raniero Cantalamessa, visiting from Italy. Pope Francis is the first bishop of Rome to have had regular and warm relationships with Evangelical and Pentecostal leaders. This closeness is reflected in the welcome given to Cardinal Bergoglio's election as bishop of Rome by a leading Argentinian Pentecostal, Dr. Norberto Saracco: "Bergoglio is a man of God. He is passionate for the unity of the church—but not just at the institutional level. His priority is unity at the level of the people."[30] It may be significant that two days after the inauguration of the ministry of the new bishop of Rome, a new Archbishop of Canterbury was enthroned as the leader of the worldwide Anglican communion. The new archbishop, Justin Welby, was early a parishioner of Holy Trinity, Brompton, and has been strongly marked by the Alpha course. But unusually for an Evangelical Anglican, he has strong Catholic connections, especially with the Chemin Neuf community. So some people are remarking that there is now a Catholic Evangelical at the head of the Anglican communion and an Evangelical Catholic as pope.[31] It is another hopeful aspect of this new season.

28. This fear, that being ecumenical means being less Catholic is treated more directly in chapter 7. In the last decade, the fraternity has been holding two international gatherings back to back, the first for bishops with member communities in their dioceses, and the second of their own leaders.

29. Comunión Renovada de Evangélicos y Católicos en el Espíritu Santo.

30. Weber, "Argentine Evangelicals."

31. See Weigel, *Evangelical*.

7

The Purification and Renewal of Identities

WHEN COMMITTED CATHOLICS BEGIN to relate to other Christians, they often have to face the fear that becoming ecumenical means being less Catholic. The more ecumenical you become, the less Catholic you will be. On the Protestant side, there can be a parallel fear, the Evangelical fear that relating positively to Catholics makes them less Evangelical.

As we shall see, this is not true for any authentic commitment to Christian unity. But it is not surprising that many Christians feel this way, because for generations patterns of formation had used such fears to reinforce their particular identity. So, for example, Catholic education had aimed at the formation of a strong Catholic identity, making Catholics wholly distinct from other Christians. So this kind of fear has often been present as the Catholic Church has opened itself to a renewal that has an intrinsic ecumenical or interchurch dimension. Popular participation in ecumenical prayer groups, in ecumenical communities, at interdenominational conferences, easily raises fears that regular sharing across church boundaries blurs church identities. It is true that in our relativistic society, many Christians have adopted a smorgasbord approach to Christian life and theology, in which they pick and choose elements they like from this source and that, so as to construct their own cafeteria form of Christian faith. This situation makes all the more urgent the formation of an authentic Christian identity that is thoroughly ecumenical. In this chapter, I focus on this question of the church identity of Catholics, particularly as it arises within a renewal seeking to build on the ecumenical grace of baptism in the Holy Spirit. From there, we need to look briefly at the related question of church loyalty. For Evangelicals, this issue is typically less a matter of denominational identity, and more an identity as a true Bible-believing Christian, but many of the following considerations apply to them too.

It may be helpful first to cite a passage from John Paul II's encyclical letter on Christian unity: "Ecumenism, the movement promoting Christian unity, is not just some sort of 'appendix' which is added to the church's traditional activity. Rather, ecumenism is an organic part of her life and work, and consequently must pervade all that she is and does."[1] This statement has to mean that being Catholic today means being ecumenical, and that not being ecumenical is not being authentically Catholic.[2] A heading in *Ut Unum Sint* sums it up: "The way of ecumenism—the way of the church."

The Challenge to be Renewed in Our Church Identities

This challenge to our church identities does not come first from the charismatic renewal. It comes from ecumenism. When we say, "Yes" to Christian unity, we accept a challenge to our church identities—more specifically to the way we understand and live our church identities. Instead of the other Christians being heretics or schismatics, they are now our brothers and sisters in Jesus Christ. This recognition already challenges how we understand ourselves as Catholics.

The ecumenical "Yes" is not just a change of tactics, but a "Yes" to the Lord's call that "all may be one." It is an "Amen" to the prayer of Jesus that "they may all be one" (John 17:21). This challenge applies equally to members of other Christian church communities with a strong sense of denominational identity, as they open themselves to this same call of the Lord. But in this chapter I focus on the challenge to Catholic identity, because of the strong emphasis in pre-conciliar teaching on the Catholic Church as the one true church, and the difficulty for many Catholics in understanding the more nuanced expression of Catholic distinctiveness since Vatican Two.

While this challenge does not arise from the character of charismatic renewal, it is often more strongly felt within the renewal, precisely because it is through the renewal that many Catholics have begun to have close

---

1. *UUS* 20.

2. Naturally, "ecumenical" here is to be understood in the sense presented in the Vatican Two decree *Unitatis Redintegratio*, and in the encyclical *UUS*.

fellowship with other Christians, and to experience them as truly brothers and sisters in the Lord.

The pastoral problem raised by this challenge from the Second Vatican Council is often heightened by the widespread Catholic assumption that we all know what a truly Catholic identity is. Then all we have to do is to protect it from confusion, and preserve it for future generations. In general, there has not been a good understanding that the whole conciliar renewal of the church calls for a renewal and a purification of Catholic identity. In the English-speaking world at least, not enough has been done to reflect on what a renewed Catholic identity would look like in an age of ecumenical dialogue and rapprochement. One consequence is that some Catholics genuinely try to be ecumenical, while trying to preserve a pre Vatican Two understanding of Catholic identity.

Key Elements in Our Shared Christian Identity

There are three foundational ecumenical convictions expressed within the documents of Vatican Two.

1. Baptized Christians of other churches and ecclesial communities are truly our brothers and sisters in Christ.

2. These Christians and their church communities are not outside the body of Christ, that is the church, but they are within; Catholic documents use the language of "imperfect communion," which is not the same as no communion.

3. What we share with other Christians is greater than what divides us.

These three convictions provide Catholics with the basis for a renewed understanding of Catholic identity within the larger Christian identity. Protestant Christians can formulate parallel convictions concerning their identity as Protestants (or as a particular kind of Protestant), and their identity as Christians.

Other Christians are Our Brothers and Sisters in Christ

Other baptized Christians are our brothers and sisters in Christ, because like us they have been born into the new life in Christ. We are brothers and sisters because we have the same Father. We are brothers and sisters because we are born of the same Holy Spirit. We are redeemed by the one Savior, and the one Holy Spirit dwells within us. As Paul wrote to the Romans, "Welcome one another, therefore, as Christ has welcomed you, for the glory of God" (Rom 15:7). In this context Paul is addressing the Jewish and the Gentile believers in Christ, but the same principle can be extended to all believers in Jesus, who are different in some way from one another.

The Other Christian Communities and Their People Are Within, Not Outside, the One Body of Christ

This existential statement is a direct consequence of our common baptism. So Paul writes, "For by one Spirit we were all baptized into one body—Jews or Greeks, slaves, or free—and all were made to drink of one Spirit" (1 Cor 12:13).[3] Note that the other Christians are not partially within the one body, even though the communion between them and us is at present imperfect. They are not partially in Christ, because the Holy Spirit does not dwell partially within them. This truth requires a radical paradigm shift of how we think of other Christian communities of faith. When we think, for example, that issues in the Catholic Church are nothing to do with Protestants, or that issues in the Anglican communion are nothing to do with Catholics, then we are engaging in the old "others outside, us inside" thinking.

What Is Shared with Other Christians Is Greater than What Divides Us

John Paul II, citing John XXIII, explicitly stated this principle.[4] This principle also follows from being brothers and sisters with a common Father. For there cannot be anything greater than the gift of faith in the triune God and in Jesus Christ, true God and true man, conferred through baptism that we share with other Christians. The words of the apostle Peter apply to all Christians: "You have been born anew, not of perishable seed but of imperishable, through the living and abiding word of God" (1 Pet 1:23). There cannot be anything greater than the gift of the indwelling Holy Spirit, also shared with other Christians. The other gifts, especially the eucharist,

3. "Through Baptism we are freed from sin and reborn as sons of God; we become members of Christ, are incorporated into the Church and made sharers in her mission." *CCC* 1213. The gift of the Holy Spirit needs to be added to this. See Acts 2:38.

4. See *UUS* 20.

that we cannot yet share, are wonderful gifts, but they flow from and follow upon faith in Jesus Christ sealed in baptism. The scandal of eucharistic division is great, because of the importance of the eucharist, and because of our common baptism.

These elements are all foundational for our shared Christian identity. There is a shared Christian identity that existed before the church divisions took place, that still exists today despite our divisions, and that will provide the foundation for the fully shared Christian identity of the one reunited church. Because Christian faith is essentially ecclesial (Christians did not come first and the church afterwards), in our state of division we are not Christians first, and Catholics afterwards. Being Catholic is not an addition to being Christian. It is our way of being Christian. As Catholic Christians we acknowledge that what unites us with other Christians is greater than what divides. So we have a Christian identity that we share with other Christians, and we have a Catholic identity that we do not yet share with them. The road to unity will increase what is shared and lessen what is not yet shared, so that we are moving towards the day when there will be no more difference between Christian identity and church identity.

The Renewal of Catholic Identity

Why is a renewal in Catholic identity necessary as a result of the Second Vatican Council? What is different about being Catholic after the council from being Catholic earlier?[5] To answer these questions, it is important to understand that throughout the history of the church, there has been a constant shaping and reshaping of the content of Catholic identity. Following the trauma of the Protestant Reformation, what it meant to be Catholic changed considerably from the medieval conception. Put simply, the wars of religion ensured that a major element in being Catholic became being anti-Protestant. The Catholic Church had to defend itself against Protestant attacks and criticisms, particularly through the development of a Catholic apologetics that refuted the Protestant objections, and provided proof-arguments for distinctive Catholic doctrines. In consequence, Catholic identity between the sixteenth and twentieth centuries was significantly shaped by those elements in Catholic teaching and practice that were rejected by the Protestants. To be Catholic was to be anti-Protestant, especially in

5. A key question for Protestant identity would be: what needs to change in Protestant identity as a genuine renewal takes place in the Catholic Church?

countries with a significant Protestant population, or regions with a history of antipathy to Catholic power structures (like Bohemia and Moravia). In the English-speaking world (but also in nations like the Netherlands, Germany, and Hungary) to be truly Catholic was to have a strong loyalty to the papacy, and to emphasize all those points on which Catholics differed from Protestants—to have a strong Marian devotion, to receive the sacraments, to have a strong devotion to the blessed sacrament (the feast of Corpus Christi became a powerful symbol of Catholic loyalty). In the same way, features identified in the popular mind with Protestantism became suspect for Catholics. A love for the Bible, and regular devotional Bible reading, were seen as Protestant, and thus not really Catholic. Church measures restricting Bible reading among lay Catholics reinforced this mentality. In a similar way, to talk about Jesus had a Protestant sound. Catholic efforts to stimulate love for the Savior typically adopted a language different from Protestant usage (e.g., our Blessed Lord, the Sacred Heart of Jesus). Any advocacy of a personal relationship with Jesus—now commonplace in the teaching of the popes since John Paul II—easily raised suspicions of not being really Catholic.

The Purification and Deepening of Catholic Identity

It is clear from the teaching of John Paul II in *Ut Unum Sint* that to be Catholic today is to be ecumenical. To ignore the ecumenical commitment of the Catholic Church is to be less Catholic, not more Catholic. The conciliar renewal requires a renewal in how we understand and live Catholic identity. Ecumenism requires a parallel renewal in identity for the Orthodox and the Protestants. For all Christians, this is a requirement of fidelity to the Lord whom we all confess.

The renewal of our identities means that we allow the Holy Spirit to reshape our identities, so that they are no longer defined by what we are against, but by *what we are for*. This means defining our identity wholly by who we are before God in Christ through the Holy Spirit. Our true identity is who we are in God's sight, personally and corporately. In the renewed understanding of the council, our identity flows first from our baptism. Thus, an authentic Catholic identity today has to be based entirely on our positive understanding of Jesus Christ and of the church.

Catholic identity is rooted in what is most basic about being part of the Catholic Church. What is most basic and distinctive for Catholics is being part of a church that is Catholic—*kat' holon*—that is, according to the whole. The idea of catholicity is connected with fullness: the fullness of divine revelation,[6] the fullness of the means of salvation, the fullness of Israel and the nations,[7] the fullness of God's purpose in his Son,[8] the fullness of Christ.[9] Acceptance of the universal ministry of the pope is essential to this identity, as the pope has the responsibility to care for the whole, to ensure the fullness, and to guard its integrity. As John Paul II has said—and this is part of renewing the papacy—"With the power and the authority without which such an office would be illusory, the bishop of Rome must ensure the communion of all the churches. For this reason, he is the first servant of unity."[10]

For Catholics, this does not mean abandoning distinctive Catholic tenets, or downplaying them because of the Protestant objections. Distinctive beliefs in the role of Mary and of the pope are still a significant part of Catholic faith, but now they need to be articulated in their full relation to Jesus Christ, showing how they belong to the apostolic heritage, and the role they play within and for the whole body of Christ. This renewal is part of the wider church renewal resulting from the return to the sources in the Scriptures of the Old and the New Testaments. Situating Catholic beliefs relating to Mary and the pope in relation to the whole faith of the church, as articulated for example in all the historic creeds, involves both a purification and deepening in the church's teaching on Mary, and on the role of the pope. This process is inseparable from a return to the biblical sources, and the deeper grounding in the biblical revelation of all Catholic doctrine, including the points of contention with other Christians.

Our Roots in the People of Israel

Just as the council's teaching on the Jewish people is an intrinsic element in the renewal of the church, so the renewal of the identities of Christians cannot ignore our relation to the Jewish people. The church's relation to the Jewish people also touches the question of Christian and of Catholic

---

6. "God graciously arranged that what he had once revealed for the salvation of all peoples should last for ever in its entirety and be transmitted to all generations." *DV* 7, cited in *CCC* 74.

7. See Rom 11:12, 26.

8. See Eph 1:10.

9. See Eph 4:13.

10. *UUS* 94.

identity. The false idea that God had rejected the Jews, and the rise of what is called replacement theology (the teaching that the church has replaced unfaithful Israel), obscured the teaching of St. Paul in Romans (11:17–24) that the Gentile believers (the non-Jews) are grafted into the cultivated olive tree (faithful Israel), and that the two (Jews and non-Jews) are to "welcome one another, therefore, as Christ has welcomed you, for the glory of God" (Rom 15:7). In Ephesians 2, the Gentile Christians are "no longer strangers and sojourners, but you are fellow citizens with the saints and members of the household of God" (Eph 2:19; compare this verse with 2:12), and so now "the Gentiles are fellow heirs [that is with the Jews], members of the same body [with the Jews], and partakers of the promise in Christ [Messiah] Jesus through the gospel" (Eph 3:6).

In his reflections on the council's teaching, Pope John Paul II spoke directly of the question of our respective Jewish and Christian identities: "Thus it [the council] understood that our two religious communities [Judaism and the Catholic Church] are connected and closely related at the very level of their respective religious identities."[11] During his visit to the synagogue in Rome in 1986, the pope developed this thought: "The Jewish religion is not 'extrinsic' to us, but in a certain way is 'intrinsic' to our own religion. With Judaism, therefore, we have a relationship which we do not have with any other religion. You are our dearly beloved brothers, and in a certain way, it could be said that you are our elder brothers."[12]

This chapter is not the place to develop this point further. But we need to note that just as the issue of the unity of the church cannot bypass the place of Israel as God's chosen covenant people, so the issue of Christian identity cannot ignore our relation to the Jewish people.

A Question of Love

How we understand our identity shapes the patterns of loyalty we develop, and that we encourage. A strong Catholic identity speaks of a strong loyalty to the Catholic Church. A strong Christian identity speaks of a strong loyalty to the person of Jesus Christ. Now of course a strong loyalty to the Catholic Church should mean a strong loyalty to Catholic teaching, with its

11. Address of John Paul II at the Vatican to representatives of Jewish organizations, March 12, 1979; see Fisher and Klenicki, *Spiritual Pilgrimage*, 4.

12. In the first-ever visit of a pope to a synagogue, John Paul II addresses the Jewish community in Rome, April 13, 1986; see Fisher and Klenicki, *Spiritual Pilgrimage*, 63.

center in the person and mission of Jesus. But we know that it is quite possible in our fallen world to have a strong institutional loyalty, not matched by a strong personal relationship with Jesus in the Holy Spirit. This directly raises the question of priorities in our loyalties, and how we understand the relationship between loyalty to the church and loyalty to Jesus.

I suggest that it is helpful to consider this question in terms of the right ordering of our loves. Central to the identity of the people of Israel is their frequent recitation of the *Shma*: "Hear, O Israel: the Lord our God is one Lord; and you shall love the Lord your God with all your heart, and with all your soul, and with all your might" (Deut 6:4–5). In the Gospels, Jesus answers a questioner by citing Deuteronomy: "You shall love the Lord your God with all your heart, and all your soul, and with all your strength, and with all your mind; and your neighbor as yourself" (Luke 10:27).

Identity leads to loyalty. Loyalty reinforces identity. Both express what we love. In the New Testament, the One God is revealed as Triune, and Jesus is revealed as the only-begotten Son of the Father, full of grace and truth (see John 1:14). So we as Christians live the first commandment by loving the one God with all our heart, soul, mind, and strength—that is to say we love the Father, the Son, and the Holy Spirit with all our being. This is the highest love.

Then we love the church. We love the church, not simply because the church brings us the gospel of Jesus, but more deeply because the church is the body of Christ, and the temple of the Holy Spirit. For a Catholic, the church is not outside my relationship to Jesus. Our becoming Christians, and our joining the church form one process. So our love for the church is not love of a religious organization (an impersonal reality—and how can you really love what is impersonal?), but part of our love for Jesus, who by his self-offering and the gift of the Holy Spirit has formed the church as his body, of which he is always the head.

Vatican Two has also opened up another dimension in our Catholic understanding of the church. There is the local (particular) church that is the diocese, and there is the universal church, that is the communion of the particular churches united with the pope, the first bishop, the primate. We can add the further dimension of the Christian family as domestic church. So love of the church is not simply love of the universal church, which more easily becomes an abstraction, but concretely the love of the local church, for the diocese, and for its expression in the local parish. This dimension also makes it easier for Catholics to relate constructively to other Christians, for whom church primarily means local church, whether the diocese (as with the Orthodox and the Anglicans), or the gathered local congregation (as with the Baptists and the Pentecostals).

8

The Purification and Healing of Memories

Ecumenism concerns the restoration of unity. The restoration of unity is impossible without deep healing. Sin poisons relationships, leading to division and disintegration. The restoration of communion between divided churches involves the healing of broken relationships. This cannot happen without the humble confession and mutual forgiveness that authentic reconciliation requires. This chapter will examine the elements necessary for reconciliation and full communion in the organic unity of the whole body of Christ, together with the potential contribution of the charismatic renewal.

Division Wounds and Weakens the Church

Today the Catholic Church recognizes that the divisions and schisms of the centuries that remain unhealed have wounded the body of Christ. So in the Catechism there is a section headed "Wounds to unity," which reads, "The ruptures that wound the unity of Christ's Body. . . . do not occur without human sin."[1] Today too we recognize that responsibility for the divisions can no longer be blamed exclusively on the other side. John Paul II has written concerning the lack of unity among Christians: "the Decree on Ecumenism does not ignore the fact that 'people of both sides were to blame,' and acknowledges that responsibility cannot be attributed only to the 'other side.'"[2]

1. *CCC* 817.
2. *UUS* 11.

Thus the ecumenical task is the healing of the wounds of divisions. It is more than the clearing up of theological disputes and the correction of doctrinal distortions, though these are necessary. We are not just dealing with mistakes, but with sin. With a mistake, one can just correct the mistake. Perhaps one needs to say, "I made a mistake." But a mere mistake does not cause a wound. Correcting a mistake does not require a change of heart. Dealing with sin is addressing a wound. The wound needs treatment. Sin requires confession of the sin for its effects to be undone. The treatment is repentance, a change of heart, a new direction. That means genuine contrition, that is, real sorrow. For this reason the church documents insist that ecumenism means conversion: "the ecumenical journey towards unity, the Second Vatican Council emphasizes above all the need for interior conversion. 'There can be no ecumenism worthy of the name without a change of heart.'"[3]

Healing the Wounds

The broken and impaired relationships between the churches resulted in the estrangement of brothers and sisters in Christ from one another, and even the refusal to recognize that they belong to the same family. Someone has to take the initiative to repair the breach. If anyone has the responsibility to repent first, it is the side that sinned first. This has often been assumed to be those who left the mother church. But large groups, even whole peoples, do not leave because everything is wonderful! So there are two reasons why it is appropriate for the Catholic Church to make the first moves towards reconciliation. The first is that normally the schisms and divisions would not have occurred if the church had acted wisely and justly before the separation. The sin in those who broke away was excessive or disordered reaction to the sin against which they were protesting. This is especially true of the Protestant Reformation. The second reason is that it is a Christian responsibility to take the first step. "But I say to you that hear, Love your enemies, do good to those who hate you, bless those who curse you, pray for those who abuse you" (Luke 6:27–28). For this reason, it is fitting that the pope, who acknowledges a pastoral responsibility for the unity of the whole body of Christ, should be the first to confess the Catholic sin.

So what is needed to heal the wounds of division? The first step is confession of the sins. In his apostolic exhortation *Tertio Millennio Adveniente* (1994), Pope John Paul II had already called for a confession of Catholic

3. *UUS* 15, citing *UR* 7.

sins in the past, including sins against unity. "Among the sins which require a greater commitment to repentance and conversion should certainly be counted those which have been detrimental to the unity willed by God for his people."[4] But before we go further, we need to address the difficulty that many people have when hearing this appeal. They will ask: "How can we repent for something that we didn't do?" These bad things happened centuries ago, so how centuries later can we be held responsible for what they did?

The Answer of John Paul II

We need to confess the sins of the past so that there can be a *purification of memories*. Unhealed memories are passed on from generation to generation: in families, in local communities, in nations, in churches. While we have personal memories, the most powerful memories are collective memories, shared by whole tribes or clans, or by an entire people. In all situations of longstanding conflict (between Orthodox Serbia and Catholic Croatia, between Hutu and Tutsi tribes in Rwanda, between Protestant Unionists and Catholic Nationalists in Northern Ireland), each side has its memories. The memories reflect their version of history. But the memories and histories of the two sides in conflict have almost nothing in common! As long as these one-sided histories continue to be passed down to the next generation, there can be no reconciliation.

Memory is the way that the past enters the present, and shapes the future. So the purification of memories requires a willingness to listen to the other side, to question our version of the history. Christians need to ask the light of the Holy Spirit to expose the biases and untruths in our story. The Jewish writer Elie Wiesel has said, "While no man is responsible for what his ancestors have done, he is responsible for what he does with that memory."[5]

Already there has been a considerable purification of memories concerning Martin Luther. Until sixty years ago, Protestant literature on Luther was almost invariably laudatory while Catholic literature was universally hostile. But today there are significant studies of Luther by both Protestants and Catholics that are recognized as fair and excellent by both sides.

4. *TMA* 34.

5. Wiesel made this statement in his speech as he presented the Elie Wiesel Foundation Humanitarian Award to King Juan Carlos I of Spain on October 7, 1991, at The Pierre Hotel in New York City.

Solidarity with Our People

As Thomas Merton said, "No man is an island." We are born into a particular family in a particular place within a particular nation. These elements form part of our natural identity. But as we grow up, hopefully we learn to accept our identity, and so begin the process of *identification*. Our education plays a major role. We learn about our people's history, our military triumphs, our culture and its language, our major writers and artists, and our heroes who embody a national spirit.

But as Christians, we also have an ecclesial identity. For most of Christian history, ecclesial identity was formed from early childhood, in the particular church heritage of parents and ancestors. But for an increasing number of Christians today, the church identity is chosen. But when we choose to join a particular church, we are entering into a history; we are receiving a heritage. So here too a process of identification begins. With Catholics, it is clear that the heritage is that of the Catholic Church. With Evangelical and Pentecostal Christians, it may be that the heritage is more that of the Evangelical or Pentecostal movements than with a particular denomination. Each Christian will know their primary faith-identification.

The purification of memories that is absolutely necessary for the healing of the wounds of Christian division depends on this faith-identification. In other words, as a Catholic I accept the history of the Catholic Church as the history of the believing people with whom I identify. We typically identify with all the positive features of our corporate history. Catholic apologetics insisted on the four marks of the church, that the church is one, the church is holy, the church is catholic, and the church is apostolic. But in marked contrast to the Old Testament presentation of Israel, very little was said about the failings, the disobedience, and the horrendous episodes in church history. As a result, we rarely identify with the negative aspects of our history, and we have difficulty in acknowledging that this also is our history.

How Important Is Social and Ecclesial Identification?

The easiest way to see the true importance of social and ecclesial identification is to understand that salvation is only possible for any human being through the total identification of Jesus—with his people Israel, and through them with all humanity. We learn about full and total identification by looking at the life of Jesus. Jesus not only identified himself with the positive side of his people (the promises given to Abraham, David, and the prophets; the Law of Moses; the feasts of Israel; the heroes of faith mentioned in Hebrews 11), but he also identified with them in their sin. We see the full identification of Jesus with his people in all its dimensions in the story of his baptism.

The baptism of John that Jesus requested was "a baptism of repentance for the forgiveness of sins" (Luke 3:3), a baptism for the people of Israel. John recognized that Jesus was without sin, so he protested, saying, "I need to be baptized by you, and do you come to me?" (Matt 3:14). But Jesus answered, "Let it be so now; for thus it is fitting for us to fulfill all righteousness" (Matt 3:15). The fulfillment of all righteousness is God's dealing with all sin and evil, so as to establish the reign of righteousness. Jesus accepts the baptism of repentance, because he is identifying with his people in their sin. He will die on the cross as sinful Israel, and so too as sinful humanity. The apostle Paul will describe this identification in graphic terms, "For our sake he made him to be sin who knew no sin, so that in him we might become the righteousness of God" (2 Cor 5:21).

How Can We Confess the Sins of Past Generations?

We recognize that we too have followed in the sinful patterns of our ancestors. This is what holy men of the Old Testament did, for example the prophet Jeremiah: "for we have sinned against the Lord our God, we and our fathers, from our youth even until this day" (3:25).[6] Even though Jeremiah was personally obedient to the Lord, and suffered for this obedience (in this he is a type of Jesus), he says without qualification, "we and our fathers have sinned." The same is true of Nehemiah (see Neh 9:32–37), and of Daniel (see Dan 9:20).

We can also confess that we have received our distorted and one-sided tribal histories, and we have gloried in them. We have often tried to defend the indefensible. Many years ago—before the Second Vatican Council—I joined the Catholic Evidence Guild, whose members spoke up for the Catholic faith in public places. The Guild, as we called it, had a handbook written by Frank and Maisie Sheed, with chapters covering all the topics dealt with from our platforms. The handbook contained answers and advice concerning all the objections made against the Catholic Church by Protestants and by nonbelievers, even having a chapter on the Inquisition.

6. See also Jer 14:20.

At no point was there any recognition that the critics might have a point, or that there was anything sinful in what we were defending. The pre-conciliar polemics and apologetics conceded no ground to the opponents. We turned the undeniable fact of bad popes into another argument for the true church: only a divinely-founded institution could survive such misfortunes. The same was true for the Protestant accusations against Catholics, depicted so brilliantly by Cardinal Newman in his lectures *The Present Position of Catholics in England,* in which his depiction of the "Prejudiced Man" still has lessons for us today.[7]

Confessing Sin as Sin

This confession has to be confession of sin that we accept as sin, and that we grieve over as sin. It is a first step to recognize that certain things done in the past were evil. This is not to judge those responsible at the time. It is a recognition of objective evil, not of subjective guilt. But there has to be a sorrow, a recognition that these things grieved the heart of God, that these were things for which Jesus died. The sorrow needs to go as deep in the psyche of those confessing as the evils being confessed entered into the hearts and psyches of their perpetrators. Otherwise the underlying evil will not be effaced.

Identifying with Sins of Our People Not Just with the Glory

As we follow the example of Jesus, our master, the formation of our identity within our people and our church will lead to an identification: "These are my people. This is my church." Here we have to cut ourselves off from the triumphalistic histories we have created for ourselves over the centuries. We identify with the evils committed by our people, as well as with their real achievements. We identify with the shame as well as with the glory. This identification requires a purification—inside us, in our hearts, and in our understanding of the past. This purification enables the real triumphs and works of grace in our heritage to be seen in their true glory, no longer mixed up with much more dubious elements.

7. See Newman, *Present Position,* 236–61.

Forgiveness

Full reconciliation between parties long in conflict requires mutual forgiveness as well as mutual confession. Normally the initiative for reconciliation comes from one side through some person or group so moved by the grace of God. In some Christian circles working for reconciliation, it is customary to follow the confession by a request for forgiveness. In my view, it is wiser and more sensitive not to make an explicit request. The granting of forgiveness requires the grace of God, and time to process the challenge of the confession made. We should allow the other party to respond as the Lord leads them when they are ready. This approach avoids the embarrassment of a silent response to our confession. This can happen, for example, when confession is made of past sins against the Jewish people (e.g., the complicity of the generation that lived through Nazism and the Holocaust). For normally the Jews will say that they are not in a position to grant forgiveness for what was done to their ancestors. They can admire and receive a Christian confession. They can thank us for it, but they cannot go further. We should deeply respect this stance.

The Rewriting of Our Histories

Some years ago the late Dr. Lukas Vischer of the WCC said that Christian unity requires that we come to a common understanding of our divided histories. There cannot be a lasting reconciliation between two sides that continue to cling to their one-sided versions of past history. In particular, this means that we have to learn to honor the heroes of both sides. This requires that we recognize what was not so holy in our heroes, as well as their genuine greatness and real achievements.

An important step on this road was opened up by John Paul II when he wrote in *Ut Unum Sint* of the importance of the martyrs for Christian unity, not just the martyrs of our tradition, but all who laid down their lives in obedience to Jesus Christ.

> All of them [all Christian traditions] in fact have martyrs for the Christian faith. Despite the tragedy of our divisions, these brothers and sisters have preserved an attachment to Christ and to the Father so radical and absolute as to lead even to the shedding of blood. . . . In a theocentric vision, we Christians already have a common martyrology. . . . I have already remarked, and with deep

joy, how an imperfect but real communion is preserved, and is growing at many levels of ecclesial life. I now add that this communion is already perfect in what we all consider the highest point of the life of grace, martyria unto death, the truest communion possible with Christ who shed his Blood, and by that sacrifice brings near those who once were far off (cf. Eph 2:13).[8]

The biggest challenge here concerns those martyrs who were killed not by Communists or Muslims, but by fellow Christians during the wars of religion.

The Contribution of Charismatic Renewal

As a movement highlighting the power and the initiative of the Holy Spirit, the charismatic renewal has much to contribute to the healing of Christian divisions and the restoration of full communion. Perhaps the biggest potential contribution can come from the heightened place of intercession in many charismatic circles over the last twenty-five years. The remarkable spread of intercessory prayer, encouraged by much popular literature, has not been much remarked upon in mainline ecumenical circles. This is partly because this development has mainly taken place in "nondenominational" or "new charismatic" circles, outside the regular ecumenical contacts, and on which there is still relatively little scholarly research and little authoritative literature. In these charismatic circles, there has been a growing realization that the sins of the past still have spiritual effects in the places of bloody conflict and merciless slaughter. The Christians who have especially picked up this challenge have been Evangelicals, discovering that such places are much harder ground for the work of evangelism today.[9] So Evangelical Christians, mostly charismatic in practice, have led the way in pioneering prayer journeys to places of major injustice (the slave ports of West Africa, the massacre sites of native peoples, the death camps of totalitarian regimes), prayer walks (especially in cities) and events like March for Jesus, proclaiming the victory of Christ publicly in the modern arena. The importance of intercessory prayer is evident in the International House of Prayer (IHOP), led by Mike Bickle in Kansas City, that is having a worldwide influence. But the Evangelical initiatives for confession and forgiveness have typically focused on the reconciliation of peoples, and

8. *UUS* 83–84.

9. See Mills and Mitchell, *Sins of the Fathers.*

have rarely been concerned with the divisions between Christians. This orientation clearly reflects the neglect of ecclesiology in Evangelical circles, and an emphasis on the true church as made up of true believers whose identities are known to God alone.

The Catholic charismatic circles that have begun to focus on reconciliation and intercession are mostly those circles that have been receptive to these Evangelical currents.[10] Some Evangelical circles are manifesting a particular openness to Catholics, as at IHOP, where the bookshop stocks a number of classic Catholic writings on prayer and spirituality. Precisely because the Evangelical–Pentecostal world has become more open to other Christians, including Catholics, through the witness of the charismatic movement, the charismatic renewal as an interdenominational current has a major potential for furthering ecumenical progress.

This potential has been clearly demonstrated in Austria, where participation by Catholics and free church Christians in the March for Jesus led to the formation in 1997 of the Round Table (*Runder Tisch*) bringing together for the first time charismatic Catholics and Lutherans, Pentecostals, free charismatics, and non-charismatic Evangelicals. This initiative is known as the *Weg zur Versöhnung* (Way of Reconciliation). Catholics from the renewal have played a major part, following the nomination in 1995 of Catholic deacon Johannes Fichtenbauer as Cardinal Schönborn's official delegate for relations with the Austrian free churches. More organized and structured than charismatic leaders meetings in other nations, the Austrian Round Table has worked in several areas, most significantly through a working group seeking to improve the legal situation of the free churches in Austria.

In France, a free charismatic church pastor, Carlos Payan, originally from Spain, a dynamic evangelist—and more surprisingly, a deeply committed ecumenist—has launched a remarkable work for Christian reconciliation. Preaching and practicing reconciliation between Catholics and the free churches for more than a decade from his base in Paris, Payan has been open to close relations with Catholic bishops. He has taken part in a public mutual foot-washing service with Msgr. Gérard Daucourt, the bishop of Nanterre in the greater Paris region, and he has written a book on Mary, which has a preface from the Primate of Belgium, Msgr. André-Mutien Léonard.

10. However, other Catholic communities have done pioneering work, most notably the Sant' Egidio community, founded in Rome.

Of huge potential significance are the initiatives for reconciliation in Latin America pioneered by Matteo Calisi and the Comunità di Gesù in Bari, Italy, through the establishment of daughter communities in Argentina and Brazil. Calisi has helped to pioneer major breakthroughs between charismatic Catholics and *los Evangelicos* (mostly Pentecostal) in Argentina and Brazil, in which Fr. Raniero Cantalamessa has played a significant role, through the establishment of CRECES.[11] In these initiatives, we can see the fruit of obedience to the leading of the Holy Spirit. Charismatic Christians bring to the ecumenical encounter an expectation of hearing the Lord, and of discerning his direction in the present situation. This openness to the Holy Spirit makes possible creative new steps forward on this road never traveled before, and that only the Holy Spirit can show.

In the reconciliation initiatives involving the confession of the sins of history, the charismatic Christian brings the experience of spontaneous expression of human feelings, and a potential facility to respond creatively to unexpected words and actions from the other parties.

But to play this creative role ecumenically, charismatic Christians need to avoid and overcome the weaknesses to which enthusiasts are often prone. There can be no over-confidence—even in the power of the Holy Spirit—no forms of spiritual arrogance on this road of humble confession. The charismatics need as much as other Christians to study and to do their homework, and to refuse the shortcut temptation that the light of the Holy Spirit renders human effort and perseverance unnecessary. Confessing the sins of the past requires a deep and accurate knowledge of the past; otherwise, inaccurate confessions can create new problems. Only those with a humble heart and a genuine feel for the complex history of nations and peoples in conflict can win the confidence of all parties.

11. The magazine *Tempi di Unità*, produced by Calisi's community, has reported this Latin American breakthrough in detail. For more on the establishment of CRECES, see also chapter 6.

9

Toward a Full Ecumenism of the Spirit

THE CHARISMATIC RENEWAL HAD an intrinsically ecumenical character from the beginning. Its central grace of baptism in the Holy Spirit was recognizably the same in the many different churches and denominations being impacted by the charismatic renewal (chapter 1). Although not envisaged by the Second Vatican Council, CCR can be seen as a fruit of the council (chapter 2). The creativity of the Holy Spirit in the renewal is demonstrated in a striking way in its ecumenical dimension (chapter 3). The ecumenical dimension raises some of the major challenges for the churches from the renewal (chapter 4). For various reasons, among them the newness of ecumenism for the Catholic Church, the early years of CCR were not a propitious time for its ecumenical potential to be realized (chapter 5). With the new developments since 1995, the wider church is now more open to the worldwide significance of the Pentecostal and charismatic movements, and to welcome these new streams into the unity conversation. In the Catholic world, John Paul II's recall to spiritual ecumenism and his new ecumenical insights can open the door for Catholics to explore the ecumenical potential of baptism in the Holy Spirit (chapter 6).

As we have considered the question of renewed Christian and ecclesial identities in the light of the ecumenical conversion of the Catholic Church at Vatican Two (chapter 7), and the need for a healing of memories for real reconciliation to take place (chapter 8), we can now piece together the elements that can characterize the charismatic contribution to the ecumenical movement. We can view this contribution as a necessary element in a newly developing ecumenism of the Spirit.

I speak deliberately of the charismatic contribution to an ecumenism of the Spirit, more than of a charismatic ecumenism, because the charismatic forms one dimension in something bigger. To make the charismatic element something in itself always produces a distortion and an imbalance. The relationship of the charismatic to the whole is treated in chapter 10. But why do I speak of an ecumenism of the Spirit rather than simply of spiritual ecumenism?

The term "spiritual ecumenism" was first used by the Abbé Paul Couturier from Lyon, France, in the mid-1930s, to describe an approach to ecumenism that was grounded in deeper conversion of all to Christ, was rooted in and nourished by prayer on the model of the prayer of Jesus in John 17, and was deeply penitent for the sins of all parties against the unity of the one body. Couturier's vision for ecumenism was adopted by the Catholic bishops at Vatican Two, and found clear expression in the decree on ecumenism.[1] John Paul II strongly endorsed the teaching of the council on spiritual ecumenism in his encyclical letter *Ut Unum Sint* in 1995.[2]

By contrast an "ecumenism of the Spirit" has not yet been widely articulated, but this phrase expresses the widespread desire for a form of ecumenism that will bridge the divide between the world of the historic churches and that of the revivalist streams (Evangelical, Pentecostal, charismatic), and that will add to the Christocentric focus of Couturier an equally strong emphasis on the role of the Holy Spirit at all stages in ecumenical work. The renewing work of the Holy Spirit in the church is wider than the charismatic renewal, but the strong awareness of the Holy Spirit in the Pentecostal and charismatic movements provides a major incentive, not only to give a more explicit place to the Holy Spirit in spiritual ecumenism, but challenges everyone to rethink the whole ecumenical task, and to develop alternative models.[3] We can say that the term "spiritual ecumenism" points primarily to approaches to Christian unity that give priority to spiritual principles, whereas the term "ecumenism of the Spirit" focuses on the initiatives and the leadings of the Holy Spirit that Christians seek to obey and follow.[4]

1. *UR* 6–8. See Kasper, *Handbook*, 10–12.

2. See *UUS* paras. 15–17, 21–27.

3. The major contribution to date comes from the Foro Pentecostal Latinoamericano in their booklet *Ecumenismo del Espíritu*. See Orellana and Campos, *Ecumenismo*.

4. The otherwise excellent book of Cardinal Walter Kasper on spiritual ecumenism (see Kasper, *Handbook*) makes hardly any reference to new initiatives of the Holy Spirit.

The hope for a new ecumenism of the Spirit can energize the ecumenical movement at all levels. Such a new ecumenism of the Spirit would be much wider than an overtly charismatic ecumenism just concerning the contribution of the charismatic renewal to unity. The renewal however makes the work of the Spirit more visible, and draws the attention of the whole church to the role of the Spirit and the charisms. In this way, what I am here calling the charismatic contribution to ecumenism will enrich the heritage of spiritual ecumenism, and it will demonstrate how an ecumenism of the Spirit presents a strong challenge to the ecumenical models and practice that have characterized the last eighty years.

What Renewal Brings to Ecumenism

I will summarize the elements that the charismatic renewal brings to the ecumenical task. In one way, this summary repeats points made in earlier chapters, but it now indicates how they are important for the work of Christian reconciliation. These elements are first briefly described, and then the rest of this chapter examines the key areas in which these elements can become operative.

Because baptism in the Spirit is the central grace of the renewal, renewal brings to ecumenism the fruit of baptism in the Spirit. Above all it is the living revelation of Jesus Christ as the reigning Lord, who since the day of Pentecost exercises his role as Lord by continually pouring out the Holy Spirit upon the church. These dimensions of revelation and spiritual power are particularly demonstrated in the spiritual gifts, to which Christians are opened up by baptism in the Spirit. Thus renewal brings to ecumenism a vibrant faith in the crucified and risen Lord, who is always exercising his lordship, so that he acts now, he speaks now, he heals now, he protects now. Here the renewal brings the experience of faith raising our understanding to the divine level, so that we can see our lives and all earthly reality as God sees them in Christ. With this experience comes a heightened expectation that the Lord will speak, that he will show the way forward, that he will act, and that he will break down the barriers.

The other huge gift that the renewal brings to the church is a freedom and spontaneity before the Lord. When we are baptized in the Spirit, our tongues are loosened, our bodies are freed to praise and to serve, we receive a freedom to be led by the Spirit in our prayer, and to express before others our heart for God, and what we receive from the Lord. In the ecumenical context, this freedom and spontaneity open up major possibilities for ecumenical sharing and deepening.

As in chapter 4 on the challenges of the renewal, I do not deal in this chapter with what the messianic Jews can bring to the search for Christian unity. As at this point the wider church has not paid much attention to the messianic Jewish movement, the charismatic movement is largely unaware of its significance. To introduce the messianic Jewish dimension here could be a distraction from showing what can be done now through grasping the ecumenical grace of baptism in the Spirit. But what the Jewish dimension can bring will remain to be addressed.[5]

Key Charismatic Principles for Ecumenism

We can now formulate a first principle to express what charismatic renewal brings to ecumenism: *do all in conscious dependence on the living lordship of Jesus Christ in and through the Holy Spirit.* This living in obedience to the living Lord requires that we acknowledge his lordship together in worship, that we feed on his Word together, that we seek his voice together, and that we obey him together. This sequence then forms the core contribution of the renewal to ecumenism.

Declare the Praises of the Lord Together

To practice this first principle requires that time be given at the outset of meetings with other Christians to a strong praise of the living Lord. We acknowledge the lordship of Jesus by declaring his resurrection victory over sin, death, and all evil, and acknowledge "Jesus Christ is Lord, to the glory of God the Father" (Phil 2:11). Declaring and singing the praises of God with zest is a hallmark of the renewal. This experience of the Spirit transforms our approach to prayer and worship. While this charismatic praise can happily include biblical psalms and traditional hymns, spontaneous praise has a capacity to lift a whole gathering to a higher realm, especially when sustained for more than a few minutes. Praise arises from faith, and stirs up faith. Praise together builds up faith together. Such praise deepens faith that in the Lord unity is possible. Together

---

5. This question is raised to some degree in chapter 11 on Mary, the church, and Israel.

we proclaim that the power of the cross is greater than the power of entrenched divisions and doctrinal conflict.

Praising the Lord together prepares our minds and our spirits to hear the Word of God together. For the Word of God to have its full effect on our ecumenical endeavors, we praise the Lord together, we hear the Word of God together, and we spend time reflecting on the Word of God together.

Feeding Together on the Word of God

The charismatic outpouring of the Holy Spirit has awakened a great love for the Scriptures as the Word of God. The Scriptures are experienced as faith-forming, and as life-giving. Just as the conciliar renewal has insisted on the first place of the liturgy of the Word, so that the sacraments cannot be rightly understood without the Word, so an ecumenism of the Spirit will give first place to the Word of God, which is for the most part a shared heritage among divided Christians.

Thus in an ecumenism enriched by the renewal, the Scriptures will be given a privileged place, because they are the Word of God inspired by the Holy Spirit. The Word of God should not be just the object of exegetical and theological discussions, but the inspiration for prayer and deep reflection together. Here it is right for all to honor the pioneering work of the Groupe des Dombes in France for the way that for over fifty years they have held together spiritual ecumenism and theological creativity.[6] In an ecumenism receptive to the gifting of the renewal, there will be a heightened expectation that the Holy Spirit will open up something from the Scriptures that will shape the direction of an ecumenical meeting.

The Word of God is food for our minds and hearts. "Thy word is a lamp to my feet and a light to my path" (Ps 119:105). As the Spirit opens us up to deeper levels of sharing, we feed on the Word of God together.

Listening Together to the Lord's Voice

Having been nourished together on the Word of God with our friends from other Christian churches, we need to hear his voice together.

---

6. Of particular importance for ecumenical reconciliation is the Groupe des Dombes document *Conversion*.

The circles familiar with the spiritual ecumenism of the Abbé Couturier will already be giving a prominence to prayer in their service of Christian unity. The renewal brings a stronger emphasis on the Holy Spirit, and will give a larger place to the explicit praise of God, Father, Son, and Holy Spirit. But often in ecumenical gatherings, the prayer element can be rather brief and formal. One opens with prayer, which can frequently be a request for God to bless the agenda already prepared, maybe put together without much prayer. However, in some gatherings of charismatic leaders from many backgrounds I have experienced a quite different pattern, beginning with extensive praise declaring the greatness of God, and the victory over all evil and darkness in the death and resurrection of Jesus. This raises the spirits, and produces an atmosphere of faith that God will act and speak here and now. Instead of asking the Lord to bless a prearranged agenda, we spend time after the praise seeking God's will for this gathering, seeking God's priorities, so that the eventual agenda will reflect the heart and priorities of the Lord. This is the way of living faith, and it produces fruit beyond our prior imagining. Much frustration is caused by going about things in the wrong order, by preparing the agenda first, and then asking God to bless it. No, the order of the Spirit is to seek the Lord first for his agenda, and then as we receive his guidance, we know it will be blessed and bear fruit. But this can only be done where there is faith that one can hear the Lord, and recognize his voice.

Obeying the Lord Together

I have had the experience several times that a listening to the Lord together has led an interchurch group to change its plans, and that this obedience to the Word that was heard produced much greater fruit than could have been imagined from the original plan. I cite one instance from the initiative Toward Jerusalem Council Two (TJCII) involving messianic Jews and Christians from many backgrounds.[7] At that time (autumn 2005), the international committee met twice each year, and was busy preparing an international prayer gathering in Jerusalem for September 2006. We had earlier decided to go to Nairobi in East Africa in the spring of 2006. But we received a clear word that we must go to Antioch before we went to Jerusalem, because the road to Jerusalem passes through Antioch.[8] We

7. On TJCII, see *Toward Jerusalem*, and www.tjcii.org.

8. Thomas Roberts, the Welsh Pentecostal (1902–1983), who served all his ministry

immediately sensed the rightness of this word, since Antioch was the first church to embody Paul's vision of the "one new man," in which Jew and Gentile are made one through the cross (see Eph 2:16; Acts 11:19–26). The resulting visit to Antioch in May 2006 was very rich and powerful. During the first session, we read aloud all the passages in the New Testament that mention the city of Antioch. After the reading, the messianic Jews recognized that three incidents damaging to the unity of the church took place in Antioch: (1) The episode when brothers from Judea insisted that the pagan converts should be circumcised in order to be saved (see Acts 15:1); (2) The controversy between the apostles Peter and Paul (see Gal 2:11); and (3) The disagreement between the partners in mission, Paul and Barnabas, concerning John Mark, the nephew of Barnabas (see Acts 15:37–39). The messianic Jews present were deeply convicted by the scandal presented to the newly-converted pagans by the Jewish believers (all involved in these squabbles were Jews), and this awareness led them to a repentance for their own lack of unity today. This heartfelt prayer was made before the cave church of St. Peter.

The Holy and the Moral

Authentic experience of the Holy Spirit always convicts of sin, of what is not holy in us and in our churches. Renewal in the Holy Spirit will expose our moral laxity, and give us a new awe of the holy God. But at the same time, the Holy Spirit will expose our legalism, and the rigidity with which we understand and apply the commandments and moral requirements of the Lord. These two different aspects of the Spirit's work indicate the practical difficulties that face divided Christians as we seek renewal and reconciliation. Only with a deep attentiveness to the Holy Spirit, and a careful listening to each other in the presence of the Lord, will progress be possible.

The ecumenical movement has already experienced that as progress has been made on centuries-old doctrinal difficulties, new tensions and obstacles have arisen in relation to ethical issues. An element in the newly-divisive issues is an elevation of contemporary experience above the objective character of the once-and-for-all revelation in the person and mission of Jesus. There has to be a shared ecclesial grappling with the challenges posed by the explosion of human knowledge, and the rapid changes in society, in

---

in France, gave a similar word in the last years of his life in relation to Constantinople and Jerusalem.

the context of a firm faith in the binding and authoritative character of the revelation of God in Jesus. This process requires the joint submission to the Word and to the Holy Spirit that characterizes an authentic ecumenism of the Spirit within committed ecclesial relationships.

Awareness that Work for Unity is a Spiritual Battle

In the churches officially committed to the ecumenical movement, there are many "northern hemisphere" Christians—even among church leaders—who do not believe that evil spirits are a force resisting the work of salvation. This pattern of unbelief, even a majority mentality in some denominations, is directly challenged by the work of the Holy Spirit in the renewal. For one consequence of baptism in the Spirit is a new or much heightened awareness of the existence of evil powers. When we come to a new knowledge of Jesus and the power of the Holy Spirit, we become aware of other spirits at work that are not holy. This pattern follows exactly the experience of Jesus, when he is driven into the desert immediately after his baptism. Being aware of the opposition of evil spiritual forces is of great importance for the work of unity. For the divisions between the churches, with all the hatred and suspicion that were generated, were both influenced by forces of evil, and then gave them more scope.

The spiritual gifts or charisms that characterize the charismatic renewal consciously equip the church once again with the "spiritual armor," of which Paul writes in Ephesians 6. We need this spiritual armor to "be able to stand against the wiles of the devil. For we are not contending against flesh and blood, but against the principalities, against the powers, against the world rulers of this present darkness, against the spiritual hosts of wickedness in the heavenly places" (Eph 6:11–12). Working for Christian unity, but ignoring this dimension of spiritual evil, normally means that the deepest roots of division are not being addressed, and the positive fruit of ecumenical labors will remain at a more surface level. An ecumenism open to the Pentecostal and charismatic movements will want to use the full range of spiritual gifts and all the spiritual armor in this battle against entrenched division that embodies institutionalized sin. Such an ecumenism will deeply respect the calling and role of intercessors who are those primarily engaged in this spiritual battle before the throne of God.

It is not helpful to think of this spiritual battle on the model of military battlefields, as though Christian soldiers march out to confront and slay demons and devils. Some popular charismatic literature about spiritual warfare has made it more difficult for intelligent Christians to take this dimension seriously. We should note that in Ephesians 6, all the armor or equipment described is defensive—breastplate (of righteousness), shield (of faith), and helmet (of salvation)—except for one item, the sword of the spirit, which is the Word of God (Eph 6:17). Jesus uses this sword of the Spirit when he repudiates the three temptations of the devil, all based on lies, by citing the Torah, in fact each time from the book of Deuteronomy. The strongholds of division are built on lies. At the heart of the spiritual battle for unity is proclaiming the truth of the Word of God against the lies, embedded in the doctrinal conflicts and the historical divisions.

The prayer of tongues can be of great value in the ecumenical context, as through it we can express something from God that goes beyond what our minds are yet able to formulate. It can be a way we let the Holy Spirit express the Lord's longing for unity: "for we do not know how to pray as we ought, but the Spirit himself intercedes for us with sighs too deep for words" (Rom 8:26). Intercession for Christian unity utilizing the spiritual gifts is a particular contribution of the renewal. Precisely because the road to a fully united church has not been traveled before, it has to be led by, and to be totally dependent on the Holy Spirit. Because we do not know how this can come about, the prayer of tongues expressing the deepest longings and groanings of the Holy Spirit for unity is a precious gift, and can take intercession for unity to a whole new level.

New Possibilities in Africa, Asia, and Latin America

I will not say much about the ecumenical possibilities in these other continents, as my experience there is very limited. However, two facts stand out that cry out to be correlated! First, the divisions between the churches are alien to the cultures and histories of the peoples of Africa, Asia, and Latin America. The divisions were imported and maintained by the European and North American missionaries, and instilled into those they trained. Second, these are the continents where Pentecostal-charismatic forms of Christian faith have had their greatest impact, and where CCR is often a major force. These two facts taken together suggest a great opportunity for a charismatic-type ecumenism to flourish where more cerebral forms make little impact. This sense is confirmed by the warm welcome given to the GCF by many Evangelical and Pentecostal leaders from these continents.

Paradoxically perhaps, the greatest openings for an ecumenism of the Spirit would seem to be in Latin America, where Catholic–Evangelical opposition has been especially strong.[9] It is significant that Argentina is the Latin American nation where real bridges have already been built between Evangelicals and Catholics, and that the future Pope Francis played a full part in those ecumenical relationships when archbishop of Buenos Aires. The phenomenon of "reverse mission," whereby the previously missionized lands send missionaries back to the old "sending-nations" could well contribute to more vibrant forms of ecumenical collaboration reinvigorating the ecumenism of Europe and North America.

The Ministry of the Pope

Pope John Paul II has already described the pope as the first servant of unity.[10] Much more will need to change in the way that the Vatican and the Catholic Church operate for this conviction to become an evident reality for other Christians. But John Paul II saw this responsibility as a necessary consequence of the Catholic convictions concerning the universal authority of the bishop of Rome. If the pope has an authority over the worldwide church directly concerned with its unity, and if this authority is understood first as a service, then the pope has the responsibility to be the first servant of unity.

This teaching of John Paul II on the papal ministry in *Ut Unum Sint* has the potential to revolutionize the practice of the papal primacy. It is in fact an application of the teaching of Jesus about authority and service: "Let the greatest among you become as the youngest, and the leader as one who serves" (Luke 22:26). Jesus presents this model of service in sharp contrast to the way that rulers exercise authority in the world. During the history of conflict and controversy between the church of Rome and other churches, the authority model of the world has been more prominent than the model of Jesus. So in the polemics following the Protestant Reformation, the Catholic Church asserted Rome's claims to universal authority, and insisted on the uniqueness of the Catholic Church. But the model of Jesus requires that having first place calls for the greatest humility, following the example of him who "though he was in the form of God, did not count equality with

9. The small book *Ecumenismo del Espíritu* comes from Latin American Pentecostal leaders involved in the GCF.

10. See chapter 6.

God something to be grasped, but emptied himself, taking the form of a servant [slave]" (Phil 2: 6–7).

What is said here about the ministry of the pope in effect applies to the whole Catholic Church in communion with Rome. When the Catholic Church makes claims about its oneness, and its unique role in the apostolic heritage, it implies a corresponding responsibility. Instead of using arguments from authority and uniqueness to separate oneself from others, advancing arguments about why we cannot do this or that, and taking a superior stance, the servant model requires that those who claim the apostolic heritage should be the first to move toward the others, the first to honor them as fellow Christians, the first to take initiatives for reconciliation. Instead of conceiving the pope's role in a conservative and defensive way, as preserving the Catholic treasure, and handing it on to future generations without contamination, we can imagine a papacy that is constantly looking for new ways of promoting unity, to open new channels for reconciliation, and to restore full communion.

If the Catholic Church can lead the way toward reconciliation and unity, Protestant communions will be less likely to succumb to the temptation to settle for forms of unity that are less than organic, and are simply forms of mutual acceptance without full engagement in one body. But for this to happen the Catholic Church has to demonstrate more clearly than in the past that unity does not mean uniformity. This is where taking the lead in mutual honoring of the work of God in the others is so fundamental.

The history of conflict and mutual alienation has caused a breakdown of trust, so that Catholic initiatives for unity, and particularly papal initiatives, are widely suspected of being cunning devices to restore Roman domination. In this situation the only Catholic initiatives that initially stand a chance of success are steps of humility that demonstrate that the age-old fears no longer have any foundation.

The Election of Pope Francis

As this text is being prepared for publication, there has been a change of pope. Following the retirement of Benedict XVI, the cardinals chose a Latin American as his successor, Cardinal Jorge Mario Bergoglio, SJ from Argentina. With this unexpected choice came the great surprise of his choice of name, Francis. From his first appearance on the balcony of St. Peter's, he referred to himself not as the new pope, but as the new bishop of Rome. He surprised the vast crowd gathered in St. Peter's Square by asking them to pray for him before giving his first blessing as bishop of Rome.

Many Christians, including Evangelicals and Pentecostals, have been hugely encouraged by the first months of the ministry of Bishop Francis of Rome with several signs of a humble spirit of service. It is clear that there is not only a change of style; there is a theology of servanthood and of ministry that undergirds his actions and decisions. Bishop Francis has a vision for "a church of the poor for the poor."[11] In his pre-conclave speech, the then Cardinal Bergoglio told his fellow cardinals, "The church is called to come out of herself and to go to the peripheries, not only geographically, but also the existential peripheries." He then warned of the dangers of a "self-referential" church: "When the church does not come out of herself to evangelize, she becomes self-referential and then gets sick. . . . The self-referential church keeps Jesus Christ within herself and does not let him out. . . . When the church is self-referential, inadvertently, she believes she has her own light; she ceases to be the mysterium lunae.[12] . . . It lives to give glory only to one another."[13] The call to go out to the peripheries has to have implications for Christian unity. It is the "self-referential" church that has no interest or zeal to go out to the others without which Christian unity cannot happen.

The deliberate emphasis that he is first chosen as bishop of Rome sends a strong signal that Bishop Francis is embracing the teaching of the council on the primacy of the pope and the collegiality of the bishops, of whom he is one. This understanding has been confirmed a month after his election by the nomination of a commission of eight cardinals drawn from all continents to serve as his permanent advisers.

But in this chapter on an ecumenism of the Spirit, maybe the most encouraging sign of all is the frequent emphasis of Pope Francis on the need to obey the leadings of the Holy Spirit. Two days after his election, the message he gave to the cardinals reveals his understanding of the Holy Spirit and Christian unity:

> Our acquaintance and mutual openness have helped us to be doc-
> ile to the action of the Holy Spirit. He, the Paraclete, is the ultimate

11. "How I would like a church which is poor and for the poor!" Address of Pope Francis to media representatives, in the Paul VI Audience Hall, Vatican City, March 15, 2013.

12. Literally, the mystery of the moon, that can only reflect the light of the sun.

13. Text made known by Cardinal Ortega of Havana, Cuba, with the agreement of Pope Francis.

source of every initiative and manifestation of faith. It is a curious thing: it makes me think of this. The Paraclete creates all the differences among the churches, almost as if he were an Apostle of Babel. But on the other hand, it is he who creates unity from these differences, not in "equality," but in harmony. I remember the father of the church who described him thus: "Ipse harmonia est." The Paraclete, who gives different charisms to each of us, unites us in this community of the church, that worships the Father, the Son, and Him, the Holy Spirit.[14]

If these words prove to be programmatic for the ministry of Bishop Francis of Rome, then a big step will have been taken toward a model for the papacy as servant of unity.

Humbling Ourselves in Common Confession

The most convincing demonstration of a transformed attitude is confession of the sins of arrogance, of lust for power, and of the recourse to coercion and violence in the past. In fact, Pope John Paul II took a number of steps in this direction. The visits to other church leaders during papal journeys have already begun a process of honoring. The call for a Catholic confession of the sins of the past, especially those against unity, has launched this process. In *Ut Unum Sint*, John Paul II brought a new clarity to the need for humble confession of our sins as church communities of faith. Ecumenical dialogue, he said, is an examination of conscience. When we meet each other consciously before God we are brought to acknowledge responsibility for our sins against unity. But the conviction of sin is a work of the Holy Spirit in each heart. As John Paul II wrote,

> Dialogue cannot take place merely on a horizontal level, being restricted to meetings, exchanges of points of view or even the sharing of gifts proper to each community. It has also a primarily vertical thrust, directed towards the One who, as the redeemer of the world and the Lord of history, is himself our reconciliation. This vertical aspect of dialogue lies in our acknowledgment, jointly and to each other, that we are men and women who have sinned. It is precisely this acknowledgment which creates in brothers and sisters living in communities not in full communion with one another that interior space where Christ, the source of the

14. Homily to the cardinals, given during the celebration of Mass in the Sistine Chapel, Vatican City, March 14, 2013.

church's unity, can effectively act, with all the power of his Spirit, the Paraclete.[15]

What does the renewal bring to John Paul II's vision of common confession of sins against unity? The renewal facilitates the "jointly and to each other" element through creating space for sharing what the Holy Spirit is showing each participant. Moreover, the freeing of emotions, not for the sake of emotionalism, but first for our own sake in enabling a deeper personal expression of sorrow, can take the ecumenical exchange to a whole new level. For Protestant Christians to see Catholics truly grieving over the wrongs inflicted on others in the past is deeply liberating, and often frees them to reciprocate at the same level.

These considerations about the role of the pope, and the confession of the sins of history, remind us that time will be needed for the wounds of division to be healed. It is a denial of the power of Jesus Christ for salvation, and of his will for unity, to say that it is impossible. But here we encounter another major difference between the ancient churches and the modern Evangelical–Pentecostal world. The ancient churches are accustomed to think in terms of centuries. Evangelicals and Pentecostals today think of the immediate. For them, one could almost say that planning for the next decade is long-term strategy. Here too we need each other. The ancient churches need the Evangelical sense of urgency, and they need the Pentecostal sense of the mighty miracle-working power of the Holy Spirit in the present. The Evangelicals and the Pentecostals need the patient realism of the ancient churches, and their deeper grasp of incarnation, of the deeply embodied character of Christian faith. All need the determination to knuckle down for the long haul. It will be another fruit of an ecumenism of the Spirit.

15. *UUS* 35.

III

Moving Toward the Fullness

10

Word, Sacrament, and Charism

THOUGH APOLOGISTS OF THE time did not admit it, the two major break-ups in church history—the schism between East and West, and the Protestant Reformation—led to an opposing of elements of divine revelation to other elements coming from the Lord, and to a consequent impoverishment of the apostolic heritage being lived by the separated bodies.

Today it is ever clearer in the Catholic Church through the Second Vatican Council, and more widely through the ecumenical movement, that the process of reconciliation and unity is one of reintegration, of rediscovery, and of recognition of the divine treasures to which the "others" bore witness, of making the body of Christ whole—in its members, in its understanding, and in its functioning. One of the clearest examples of this reintegration is the recognition that Word and sacrament belong together. After the Reformation when the Word of God became the banner of the Protestants, and the Bible was used in a polemical way against Catholics, Catholics focused on the beliefs that Protestants denied—primarily eucharistic sacrifice, papal authority, and Mary. One result was a tension between Word and sacrament that lasted for four hundred years. Catholics devoted to the Bible were easily accused of Protestant sympathies, and Protestants appreciating sacrament could likewise be suspected of crypto-Catholic tendencies.

The Lord's main instrument in correcting this false antithesis was the movement for liturgical renewal. Because the Bible is central to the liturgy of the church, the liturgical pioneers of the early twentieth century, like

Lambert Beauduin (Belgium) and Pius Parsch (Austria), worked to open up the Bible to the Catholic people, and to make the liturgy truly participative. So, for example, Parsch formed the first Catholic Bible study groups after the First World War. The Second Vatican Council fully embraced the liturgical renewal, which had been most vigorous in continental Europe north of the Alps. In the constitution on the liturgy, the bishops stated: "Sacred scripture is of the greatest importance in the celebration of the liturgy. . . . It is from scripture that the petitions, prayers and hymns draw their inspiration and their force, and that actions and signs derive their meaning."[1] So the renewal of the liturgy has involved a restoration of the essential role of the Word of God, including the homily as an integral "part of the liturgical action," that relates "proclamation of the Word of God to the sacramental celebration and the life of the community."[2] An essential element in this restoration has been the removal of all restrictions on Catholic Bible-reading—measures that had arisen from the fear of people turning Protestant—with the council's declaration: "Access to sacred scripture ought to be widely available to the Christian faithful."[3]

As a fruit of the conciliar renewal, official Catholic documents today insist that Word and sacrament belong together. The Word always comes first, but then the Word becomes flesh. Both are needed for the life of the church: the proclamation of the Word, and the sacramental celebration of the Word become flesh. Without the proper rooting in the Word, faith easily degenerates into something abstract or ideological (among the educated) or into superstition (among the less educated).[4] Without the bodily communitarian expression of Word in sacrament, something is lacking by way of historical rooting and intergenerational communication.

1. *SC* 24.

2. See Benedict XVI, *Sacramentum Caritatis*, 46.

3. *DV* 22.

4. See the famous remark of Blessed John Henry Newman, when he warned against the danger of a passive laity: "when she [the church] cuts off the faithful from the study of her divine doctrines and the sympathy of her divine contemplations, and requires from them a *fides implicita* in her word, which in the educated classes will terminate in indifference, and in the poorer in superstition." *Consulting*, 106.

The Contribution of the Charismatic Renewal

One major contribution of the charismatic renewal to the bringing alive of Word and sacrament has been a love of the Scriptures as the Word of God received through baptism in the Spirit. This outpouring of the Spirit has probably done more to make ordinary Catholics avid readers of the Bible than any courses of biblical studies. As we know, important decrees issued by church authority do not immediately change the hearts and practices of the faithful. For this, a breath of the Holy Spirit is needed; the Spirit who changes hearts, and implants new desires. At the same time, some new ecclesial movements, such as the Community of Sant' Egidio, Focolari, and Communion and Liberation, have done much to encourage Bible reading and study among their members. In this process of opening up to the riches of the Scriptures, the ecumenical dimension of the renewal made a notable contribution: for in the early years some of the most popular teachers at Catholic Renewal events were Protestants, who had years of soaking in the Word behind them. In more recent times, some new Catholics who brought with them a deep love of the Word from their Protestant formation have played an important role in the scriptural formation of Catholics.[5]

The charismatic outpouring of the Spirit has also freed Christians to express their faith and worship through gestures and bodily movements. So charismatic Christians typically raise their arms in worship, prostrate themselves in adoration, are ready to dance, to move in procession, and to clap their hands in acclamation of the Lord. This dimension of the renewal has facilitated the reintegration of Word and sacrament, by bringing together in practice the physical and the spiritual, thus undermining from within any tendency to regard all ritual and outward expression as inherently unspiritual. In this way, the renewal has helped to open Evangelical Christians to liturgy, and among Catholics has supported the conciliar renewal's holistic vision of the human person and society.

The renewal has also contributed to a deeper awareness of the role of the Holy Spirit in the liturgy. At the scholarly level, the role of the Holy Spirit was enhanced in the council documents through the contributions of Eastern Catholic bishops and of the Orthodox observers. The awakening of praise in the hearts of the faithful has been a hallmark of the renewal, and the experience of baptism in the Spirit often leads to the discovery of

5. A well-known example is Scott Hahn, who teaches in the Franciscan University of Steubenville, Ohio. Less known, though much loved in the British Isles, is David Matthews, originally from Northern Ireland.

the eucharist as the great act of praise and thanksgiving. The new freedom to use one's body in the worship of the Lord finds a natural context in the worship of the liturgy. The liturgy in turn serves as a school to channel charismatic exuberance into dignified community worship, in which the individual worshiper is being drawn into the corporate worship of the church as body of Christ.

The Charisms

However, when considering the contribution of the charismatic renewal, a major place has to be given to the restoration of the charisms. In this context, restoration means a bringing again into the regular life of the church. When we consider the charisms most characteristic of the renewal (those listed in 1 Cor 12:8–10), we cannot say that they were simply absent from the church in past generations. But insofar as such gifts were manifest, they were not understood in an ecclesial context, but as individual signs of the holiness of particular people or places. What has been distinctive not just of the renewal, but first of the Pentecostal movement, was the recognition that these gifts belong to the Holy Spirit's equipment of the church so that she can fulfill her mission. For the Pentecostals, it was the empowering by the Spirit to take the full gospel to the ends of the earth before the Lord comes.

A huge step forward in the church's understanding took place at Pentecost 1998, when John Paul II addressed all the new ecclesial movements and communities. The pope was clearly seeing this new dynamism of the Holy Spirit in the Catholic Church as a fruit of the Second Vatican Council. Indeed, he went so far as to say, "This was the unforgettable experience of the Second Vatican Ecumenical Council during which, under the guidance of the same Spirit, the church rediscovered the charismatic dimension as one of her constitutive elements."[6] In recent times, particularly in the pontificate of Benedict XVI, there has been much Catholic discussion about the right interpretation of Vatican Two, with talk about renewal and reform, rupture or continuity.[7] In this context, this address of 1998 makes a big claim for the radical transformation that took place at the council. For John Paul II continued: "The institutional and charismatic aspects are co-essen-

6. Address of John Paul II, Ecclesial Movements, para. 4.

7. Benedict XVI spoke primarily about a hermeneutic of renewal, opposing a hermeneutic of rupture, asserting the continuity between the pre-conciliar and the post-conciliar.

tial as it were to the church's constitution. They contribute, although differently, to the life, renewal and sanctification of God's people. It is from this providential rediscovery of the church's charismatic dimension that, before and after the council, a remarkable pattern of growth has been established for ecclesial movements and new communities."[8] The rediscovery of the charismatic dimension can hardly be a minor adjustment!

It is evident that the charismatic dimension of the church is much wider than the charismatic renewal. But this recognition does not mean that the renewal had nothing to do with the new awareness of the charismatic within the church. For the charismatic renewal highlights the character of the charismatic, and makes it more clearly visible: the unpredictability of its appearance, its unmediated nature as coming forth directly from the risen and glorified Lord, its tangibility, and its impact upon the human heart.

The Institutional and the Charismatic

The words of John Paul II are of great importance for understanding the significance and place of the renewal, and of baptism in the Spirit in the life of the church. What is it that distinguishes these two dimensions, the institutional and the charismatic? First, the institutional element is that which goes back uninterruptedly to the origins of the church, and that is grounded in the earthly ministry of Jesus. The institutional element is that which has to be present in every age and generation for there to be church at all. Such an approach is theological, not sociological. For the heart of the institutional is not the bureaucratic or organizational apparatus of any epoch, but the basic structural elements coming from the church's foundation. In other words, the heart of the institutional is Word and sacrament, including the basic ministerial structure of the episcopate, gathered around the successor of Peter. These elements are always present in the church.

The charismatic dimension by contrast is unpredictable, it comes and it goes, and it cannot be planned. It does not necessarily take the same form in different epochs; indeed, we can say it will never simply replicate earlier charismatic outbreaks. But the charismatic is poured out upon the historic body—to challenge, purify, enliven, and redirect. When the charismatic is not rightly related to the institutional, it cannot realize its full purpose, and it will be lacking in historical rooting. However, this is not saying that charismatic elements outside the historic structures are

8. Address of John Paul II, Ecclesial Movements, para. 4.

inauthentic and false; it is saying that they lack their proper context for bringing forth their full long-term fruit.

The institutional-charismatic distinction enables us at the same time to emphasize the fundamental character of the sacrament of baptism, as well as the providential and transformative character of the charismatic action of the glorified Lord, who baptizes with the Holy Spirit. Without a deepened understanding of the sacrament of baptism, one cannot grasp the importance of being baptized in the Spirit for the church of our time. Thus the affirmation of both elements, the institutional and the charismatic, is essential for upholding realities that belong to different ecclesial categories, in order to avoid the subordination of the charismatic to the institutional (Catholic tendency) and the exaltation of baptism in the Spirit at the expense of sacramental baptism (Pentecostal tendency).

In the light of these comments, we can see that the charismatic renewal, along with its defining characteristics, baptism in the Spirit and the charisms, is of its nature a charismatic reality. In the way that we know the renewal, it is a phenomenon of the twentieth and the twenty-first centuries. There have been charismatic currents before in Catholic history (the monastic movement, the Franciscans, the Devotio Moderna, etc.), but they have not taken this form. To recognize the renewal as a charismatic development in our days frees us from all attempts to read back an identical baptism in the Spirit into previous periods of the church, and it frees us from the unhistorical attempt to demonstrate that all the canonized saints were really charismatic in this sense. In particular, it shows that the constant Catholic attempts to define baptism in the Spirit solely in terms of the sacraments of initiation is based on a category mistake; we are dealing with quite distinctive realities that need to come together, but in full respect of the distinctive character of both.

Another point that should be noted flows from the ecumenical character of the charismatic outpouring of the Spirit. The renewal is clearly the same work of the Holy Spirit being liberally poured out in very different ecclesial and theological milieux. The attempt to define baptism in the Spirit by fitting it firmly into a Catholic framework has the unintended consequence of undermining the fundamental unity of the Spirit being poured out. When, for example, a charismatic Baptist cannot identify with a sacramental Catholic definition of baptism in the Spirit, what are we to say? First, that both Catholic and Baptist need with the aid of the Holy Spirit to relate this grace to their own heritage. But secondly, they need to avoid elevating their understanding to the level of another doctrine that divides. As they both allow this grace to challenge, purify, and enliven their ecclesial life, they will find that it will draw them closer, and begin to heal the wounds of separation.

Word, Sacrament, and Charism

Now we can come to a major challenge of the Pentecostal and charismatic movements to the ecumenical movement in its current expressions and self-understanding. This chapter started from the modern ecumenical recognition of the full complementarity of Word and sacrament. But the massive spread of Pentecostal and charismatic forms of Christian faith, especially in the last fifty years, and above all in Africa, Asia, and Latin America, challenges the idea that Word and sacrament are enough. There is a third element: charism. Church is not fully church, and operating with all the endowments of the Lord without Word, sacrament, and charism.

Is there a contradiction in saying that the church needs Word, sacrament, and charism and understanding the charismatic dimension of the church as that which comes and goes as the Holy Spirit determines? If the charismatic dimension is co-constitutive of the church, is it not needed all the time? Perhaps the difference between the permanent (institutional) and the occasional (charismatic) can be illustrated in this way. Word, sacrament, and ordained ministry are permanent gifts of the Lord to the church; they are transmitted from generation to generation. The charismatic is not passed on in this way to the next generation, but is poured out by the risen Lord as he wills; it has to be received in the form in which it is given at that time and in that place. The church is always in need of the charismatic breath, because the church lives by the Holy Spirit sent by the Father through his Son; but the form this gift takes cannot be predicted. Experience of the charismatic then enables the church to live the permanent endowments of the church (Word, sacrament, and ordained ministry) as gifts of the Lord animated by the life-giving Spirit.

Of course, ever since the beginning of the charismatic renewal in the historic churches, and especially those with a liturgical heritage, participants in the renewal have been faced with the question of how to receive and integrate the charisms into the life of the church. By now they can draw upon nearly fifty years of experience. However, the question is not simply how to make an occasional introduction of charisms into church liturgy or parish practice, but how to give a practical sovereignty to the Holy Spirit in the way that we live church. We are accustomed to organizing church life on the basis of Word and sacrament (that includes ordained office), but we are not accustomed to submitting our ways to the sovereign Lord, who directs and speaks to his people through charismatic gifts.[9]

We can perhaps best illustrate this challenge by drawing attention to the statement in Ephesians 2:20 that the church is "built upon the foundation of the apostles and prophets." We can see this as a New Testament formulation of the complementarity of the institutional and the charismatic. We should not make the mistake of assuming that the "prophets" here refer to the Old Testament prophets. These prophets are clearly New Testament prophets, a point that is confirmed in chapter 4 where "his gifts were that some should be apostles, some prophets, some evangelists, some pastors and teachers" (Eph 4:11). See also the description of the church at Antioch, "Now in the church at Antioch there were prophets and teachers" (Acts 13:1).

How are charisms to be given greater recognition and scope in the church? While encouragement from the pope and senior church leaders is very important—especially for confirming its rightness—the working out of new patterns almost certainly has to come from below, rather than being recommended or imposed from above. Such a work has to be led by the Holy Spirit, who blows where he wills. Maybe a group of bishops will recognize the prophetic character of some church member, lay or ordained, and open up space for their gifting, without necessarily conferring any new titles. This is most likely to happen where ordained leadership listens together to the Lord in humble faith, expecting that the Lord will speak in his good time. Here a passage from the Vatican Two decree on the ministry and life of priests will be highly relevant: "While testing the spirits to discover if they be of God, they [priests] must discover with faith, recognize with joy, and foster diligently the many and varied charismatic gifts of the laity."[10]

A Distinctive Contribution of Charismatic Renewal

The bringing together of Word and sacrament has been a fruit of liturgical and theological studies in church circles open to and participating in the

9. There was a remarkable instance of charism influencing church leadership on January 1, 1901, when Pope Leo XIII consecrated the twentieth century to the Holy Spirit at the persistent suggestions of an Italian nun, Elena Guerra.

10. *PO* 9.

ecumenical movement. The integration of charisms into the overall picture will require a major contribution from the Pentecostal and charismatic movements. This is only likely to happen as these movements interact with and participate in the overall ecumenical rapprochement, and as the liturgical churches take seriously these newer movements of the Spirit. That is why some of the more recent developments described in chapter 6 are particularly significant. The increasing attention being given to ecclesiology by Pentecostal theologians also makes an important contribution.[11]

Meanwhile, those in the renewal need to acknowledge a special responsibility as those to whom the character and the importance of the charismatic element has been made known with a particular clarity. That is to say, renewal leaders need to ensure that in the way their meetings are conducted, the charisms are given full scope and encouragement. This will not only provide a model for the wider church, but it will invigorate the renewal and deepen its impact. This role requires a humility, avoiding all self-advertisement, and focused on faithful obedience to the Lord. Leaders do not proclaim, "We are the model," but live their giftings in a way that the model character is evident to all.

11. See Kärkkäinen, *Ecclesiology*; and Chan, "Mother-Church."

11

Mary, the Church, and Israel

EVER SINCE THE PROTESTANT Reformation, the role of Mary has been one of the most difficult and sensitive issues in Catholic-Protestant relations. The difficulties are at their most acute in the encounter between Catholics and Christians with an Evangelical heritage. If the Evangelical-Catholic encounter is to have any chance of lasting fruit, the Mary issue cannot be avoided.

Due to Protestant opposition to all invocation of Mary and the saints as being incompatible with the unique mediation of Jesus Christ, devotion to Mary became one of the hallmarks of Counter Reformation Catholic identity. Over the next four hundred years, it seemed as though the obstacles to understanding and fellowship in this area just kept multiplying. The flourishing of Marian devotions, an increasing number of Marian apparitions and pilgrimages, the solemn definition of the two Marian dogmas (the Immaculate Conception in 1854, and the bodily Assumption in 1950), plus forms of consecration to Mary, personal and national, often reflected a spirit of Catholic triumphalism, and of anti-Protestant polemics. To the Protestant it looked like proof of the unbiblical and sub-Christian character of Roman Catholicism.

This background helps to underline the remarkable progress in interchurch relations over the past fifty years since the Second Vatican Council. One decision in particular greatly helped this progress: the decision to include the teaching on Mary within the constitution on the church. This proposal gave rise to the most emotive debate, and led to the closest vote of the whole council.[1] The inclusion of the teaching on Mary within a Christocentric vision of the church sent a strong signal to other Christians of a Catholic desire to build bridges and to reduce the tensions provoked by a Marian teaching that was not properly related to the whole corpus of Catholic doctrine.

But despite the progress that has been made since the 1950s through Vatican Two and mainline ecumenical dialogues, Mary remains a highly emotive point of opposition, particularly in Catholic relations with Evangelical and Pentecostal Christians, who have largely remained outside the ecumenical movement. But these are the Christians with whom positive faith-based relationships have been made possible, largely through the charismatic renewal. These difficulties were vividly illustrated at a workshop on unity I gave to a Youth With A Mission leaders conference in 1993, at which I decided to tackle the issue of Mary head on. Toward the end, one participant made a very perceptive observation: that Mary was a doctrine that Protestants denied, while Mary was a person whom Catholics loved.

The issue of Mary shows us that the Spirit's work of renewal is not just about bridging the gaps in Catholic-Protestant understanding, but it is bringing together what had become separated in various ways within the totality of Catholic faith. Renewal means reintegration, the reconnecting of all dimensions of Christian faith to the biblical and christological foundations within the unity of the mysteries of faith. The authentic wholeness of the church's faith is carried through the centuries by the ancient liturgies that span both time and space. This reintegration is inseparable from thorough-going liturgical renewal.

Through the ages, we can see that in the Western church Mary became to some extent independent of Jesus, and independent of the church. This trend is illustrated by the appearance of statues of Mary without the Christ-child, in contrast to the iconography of the Eastern church, that always depicts mother and child together. We can see it in the rise of mariology as a distinct theological science, disconnected from Christology and ecclesiology. This separation made possible forms of Marian piety that imply that the heavenly mother understands our human problems better than a solemn and more remote Son of God—thus indicating a serious failure to understand the incarnation, the central tenet of Christian faith. These tendencies promoted an image of Mary up there in heaven alongside Jesus, while the church was down here with us. All such developments increased

1. The bishops decided for inclusion by 1,112 votes against 1,072.

the gap and the disconnect between Catholic and Protestant at the level of Christian empathy and fellow-feeling.

The Major Breakthrough at Vatican Two

The separation of Mary from the church was corrected in principle at Vatican Two with the decision to include the teaching on Mary as a chapter within the constitution on the church, rather than to have a separate schema *De Beata Virgine Maria*. This decision intended that the teaching on Mary be biblically-grounded, and would conform to the christocentric and pneumatological emphases of the council. It reconnected the teaching on Mary to the patristic roots, and to the tradition of the Eastern church in seeing Mary as "eschatological icon of the church."[2]

The integration of Marian teaching and piety into the full life of the church Catholic has been further promoted by the encyclical letter *Redemptoris Mater* of Pope John Paul II (1987), in which he says, "The Second Vatican Council, by presenting Mary in the mystery of Christ, also finds the path to a deeper understanding of the mystery of the church."[3] Placing Mary within the mystery of the church enriches our understanding of both Mary and the church. John Paul II takes up a key idea from *Lumen Gentium* of the church as "pilgrim church" within history and speaks of the Mother of God at the center of the pilgrim church (Part 2). This context enables the pope to raise the issue of Christian unity: "The journey of the church, especially in our own time, is marked by the sign of ecumenism."[4]

The teaching of Vatican Two has since been gathered and ordered in *The Catechism of the Catholic Church* (1994). The teaching on Mary is almost all found in Part 1, which expounds the Apostles' Creed. The teaching on the virginal conception and birth of Christ is presented in chapter 2 on the Son; the greater part of the teaching on Mary is given in chapter 3, on the Holy Spirit under article 9: "I Believe in the Holy Catholic Church." The reintegration of Mary into the mystery of the church is here most explicit, with the sixth paragraph being entitled "Mary—Mother of Christ, Mother of the Church."[5]

---

2. This is the heading of a subsection in *CCC* 972.

3. *RM* 5.

4. *RM* 29.

5. *CCC* 963–75.

The Breakthrough Still Needed

But the separation of Mary from the body of the church was not the first such separation. There was an older separation that began the process of detaching Mary from her biblical rooting, and that has contributed strongly to the ecumenical tensions concerning the person and role of Mary. It is the separation of Mary from her own people, the people of Israel. Here the most serious distortion was caused by cutting Jesus himself off from his roots in Israel, along with turning the twelve into universal apostles without any particular calling to Israel, or anchoring in their own people.

All these tendencies to distance the church and her faith from the roots in Israel are contested by the conciliar acknowledgment that God has not rejected the Jewish people: "God holds the Jews most dear for the sake of their fathers; he does not repent of the gifts he makes or of the calls he issues."[6] A later Vatican document would make this much more explicit: "We must . . . rid ourselves of the traditional idea of a people punished, preserved as a living argument for Christian apologetic. It remains a chosen people, 'the pure olive on which were grafted the branches of the wild olive which are the gentiles.'"[7] This recognition requires that the church reexamine her roots, re-receive everything authentic from the beginnings in Israel and be purified of all that resulted from our self-alienation from the origins. This process has to begin by receiving the full Jewishness of Jesus, and the full Jewishness of Mary. It is enormously helped and stimulated by contact with messianic Jews, for whom it is axiomatic that the whole first generation of disciples were Jewish, and that the New Testament is mostly the work of Jewish believers in Jesus.

Mary's Role in the Birth of the Church

The desire to provide a stronger biblical foundation for the role of Mary has led to greater recognition of Mary as the first believer in her Son. This faith in her Son dates from the annunciation, when Mary gave her full assent to the word and promise of the angel that "the child to be born will be called holy, the Son of God" (Luke 1:35). Here we find the beginnings of the church, wholly within Israel. At this point there is no rupture. There is simply an expansion within the messianic hope of Israel.

6. *NA* 4.

7. Commission, *Notes*, 25.

However, even in the infancy gospels, there are clear pointers that the coming of "the Son of God" will provoke opposition, and even divide God's people. The most explicit warning comes from the old man Simeon, who was "looking for the consolation of Israel" (Luke 2:25). He tells Mary, "Behold, this child is set for the fall and rising of many in Israel, and for a sign that is spoken against" (Luke 2:34), adding that "a sword will pierce through your own soul also" (Luke 2:35). Catholics have customarily interpreted this soul-suffering of Mary as the agony of watching her son die the terrible death of crucifixion. But by forgetting the Jewishness of Mary, we have missed the obvious connection between the first and second parts of Simeon's prophetic utterance. Surely the future suffering of Mary has something to do with "the fall and the rising of many in Israel."

In this perspective, the suffering of Mary has at its heart seeing her son, Messiah and Son of God, being rejected by his and her own people. This suffering has something in common with Paul's anguish expressed in Romans, "I have great sorrow and unceasing anguish in my heart" (Rom 9:2), because of the unbelief of his fellow Jews. It is a sundering of the bonds that unite the people of Israel, a sundering within the heart of Mary, who totally loves and accepts her Son, and who is totally committed to her own people, holding firm to God's promises and covenants. "He has helped his servant Israel, in remembrance of his mercy, as he spoke to our fathers, to Abraham and to his posterity for ever" (Luke 1:54–55). At the foot of the cross, Mary somehow already experiences within her the schism within Israel, between those who accept her Son (beginnings of the church), and those who reject him (beginnings of Judaism), for she remains deeply connected to both.

As the first Jewish disciple of the Messiah of Israel, who will become the Savior of the world, Mary represents faithful believing Israel. As the first believer in her son, who is soon joined by other faithful Israelites like Elizabeth, Zechariah, Joseph, Simeon, and Anna, Mary is at the heart of this nascent church. This infant Jewish church is founded in the reality of the incarnation, before Jesus ever begins his public ministry. At the origins of this embryonic church John the Baptist was sanctified in his mother's womb, and she cried out, "Blessed is she who believed that there would be a fulfillment of what was spoken to her from the Lord" (Luke 1:45). We can say that in Mary, faithful Israel is becoming church. Through the challenges that Mary faces in faith throughout the life of her Son, especially its climax in his passion, death, and resurrection, God was prophetically and proleptically transforming Israel into church.

Seeing the church as grounded in the incarnation makes clearer its totally relational character. This relational character is further demonstrated in the gathering of disciples around Jesus from the start of his public ministry. The church is first communion centered in Jesus, before it becomes an institution. The institutional element comes later to structure a reality that already exists, starting with the call of the twelve, and their introduction into the mission of Jesus. The choice of the twelve shows that they will be the leaders of this transformed Israel: see Matt 19:28; Luke 22:30; Rev 21:12,14, passages that all connect the twelve apostles with the twelve tribes of Israel.

The opening up of the gospel to the nations (Gentiles, *goyim*) happens as a consequence of the death and resurrection of Jesus. Although some gospel episodes foreshadow the coming of the Gentiles to faith, the mission of Jesus during his earthly ministry was limited to "the lost sheep of the house of Israel" (Matt 15:24), as were the mission journeys of the twelve (Matt 10:5–6). The "great commission" to "go therefore and make disciples of all nations" is only given by the risen Jesus after the completion of his earthly ministry (Matt 28:19). For this to become a reality required the extraordinary call of Saul of Tarsus, from outside the ranks of the twelve, to be "the apostle to the nations." It is the apostle Paul, who will clearly articulate the vision of the church as the union of Jew and Gentile in one body, reconciled through the cross (Eph 2:14–16), and who will teach that Gentiles come to salvation by entering "the household of God, built upon the foundation of the apostles and prophets, Christ [Messiah] Jesus himself being the cornerstone" (Eph 2:19–20). In context, comparing verses 19–22 (the condition of the Gentiles after coming to Christ) with verse 12 (their previous condition), it is not the Jews who leave Israel and join the church, but the Gentiles who are brought into "the commonwealth of Israel" (see Eph 2:12), so that they are now "fellow heirs, members of the same body, and partakers of the promise in Christ Jesus through the gospel" (Eph 3:6). Paul describes this as "the mystery of Christ" (Eph 3:4).

Increasingly as the Christian churches and faith communities have acknowledged that God has not rejected the Jewish people, and that they remain the chosen covenant people, there has been a turning away from speaking of the church as the "new Israel," meaning or assuming that the church as new Israel has replaced the Jewish people, understood to be the "old Israel." In fact, *Lumen Gentium* is not entirely free from this language, probably because the formulation of *Nostra Aetate* came later in the council.[8] This phrase "the new Israel" is not found in the New Testament, and this replacement concept cannot be what is meant by "the Israel of God" in Gal 6:16.

The Importance of Mary for Unity

We have sought to replace Mary in her Jewish context and to see her, the first believer in her Son, as the embodiment in her person of the church to be formed out of and within Israel. Now we are ready to understand how Mary is a key link between the two Testaments, and the key link between Israel and the church. Because Jesus did not have a human father, he receives his humanity, which for him is his Jewishness, totally from Mary and from the Holy Spirit. Mary is thus a unique bridge between Israel and the church.

But we should not think of this bridge as connecting two realities that are totally different. We have thought of Christianity and Judaism in this way, because of the painful history of separation and mutual rejection. Mary could never have thought in this way. The separation that began in her lifetime was at the heart of the sword that pierced her soul. Mary is the bridge, rather in the sense that she is an Israelite and a Jew, who fully received into her Israelite faith the messianic fulfillment embodied in her Son. She represents in her own being and faith the right relation between Israel and church, between the covenants with Israel and the new covenant in the blood of Jesus. The removal of all anti-Semitism, of all anti-Judaism, of all replacement thinking concerning church and Israel, will free all Christians to receive a fully biblical vision of Mary, as well as a fully biblical vision of her Son. In this healing of the separation of the church from Israel, the witness of Jewish believers in Jesus is essential, alongside the purified faith of Christians from all backgrounds and traditions.

8. "Just as the people of Israel in the flesh, who wandered in the desert, were already called the church of God, so too, the new Israel, which advances in this present era in search of a future and permanent city, is also called the church of Christ." *LG* 9 c. Earlier in para. 9, we find this wording: "it [the church made up of Jew and Gentile] would be the new people of God." 9 a.

The Woman of Revelation 12

With this return to the Jewish roots, we can understand the vision of John in the book of Revelation in a way that is not divisive. Catholics have often understood Mary to be the "woman clothed with the sun, with the moon under her feet, and on her head a crown of twelve stars" (Rev 12:1). So this passage is used in the Roman liturgy of the feast of the Assumption of the Blessed Virgin Mary on August 15. By contrast Protestant exegetes have typically understood the woman to be Israel or Jerusalem. But this choice—Mary or Israel-Zion—is unnecessary. We can understand the woman to be Israel-Zion, from whom will come the Messiah-King who will be born of this particular Israelite woman, Miriam or Mary.

It is clear that the son of the woman "who is to rule all the nations with a rod of iron" (Rev 12:5) is the Messiah spoken of in Psalm 2 (Rev 12:5 is echoing Ps 2:9) in which the Lord says, "I have set my king on Zion, my holy hill" (Ps 2:6). So the woman who gives birth to this male child has to be in a literal way the mother of the Messiah. But this woman who is Israel-Zion, embodied in Mary, then has offspring, "those who keep the commandments of God and bear testimony to Jesus" (Rev 12:17). This phrase may have had the Jewish disciples particularly in view, as those who both observed Torah, and believed in Jesus. In any case, the woman here has become the church. In other words, this chapter can be understood as describing the transformation of Israel–Zion personified in Mary as mother into Israel-Zion-Church, also personified in Mary as mother.

The Way Ahead

The reintegration of Mary into the church has already made possible constructive ecumenical discussion about the mother of the Lord. This reintegration has itself been made possible by a return to the biblical roots and to the patristic heritage. This process has been taking place within the churches committed to the ecumenical movement, and particularly within those honoring the patristic as well as the biblical witness.[9] At the present time, much more progress has been made in the realm of Catholic theology and official teaching, than in the spheres of popular piety and spirituality.

9. One of the most remarkable ecumenical documents on Mary comes from the Groupe des Dombes in France: *Mary in the Plan of God.*

But such a lag is normal. Longstanding and deep-rooted practices are not changed overnight by official decree.

The further step of the reintegration of Mary into Israel is almost certainly the only way to bridge the Marian gap between Catholics and Evangelicals. This is because it depends on a deeper penetration of the Scriptures and of the Jewish world in the inter-testamental and New Testament periods. Evangelicals and Pentecostals receive this more easily because it depends on what is biblical, and not on the later evidence from the fathers of the church, all of whom in effect embraced the idea that the church had replaced Israel. As mentioned, the messianic Jews can be a real help to the extent that they can free themselves from Evangelical presuppositions that are incompatible with the Israelite-Jewish heritage, such as an antipathy to liturgical forms and a deep suspicion of tradition.

What is the responsibility of CCR in this question? There is much evidence to show that it is the charismatic movement that has opened the doors to better relations between Catholics and Evangelicals. CCR has helped to present a different face of the Catholic Church, and to provide an experience of shared fellowship in Christ. But to date, the main contribution of CCR to resolving the difficulties concerning Mary has been indirect, through its undoubted exaltation of the person of Jesus. But there needs to be confession that in some places, CCR has exacerbated the difficulties by an inadequate way of relating the distinctive gifting of the renewal to the Catholic tradition. In relation to Mary, it is not sufficient to introduce some charismatic elements into unrenewed patterns of Marian piety, that owe little to Scripture, and that have become disconnected from the Trinitarian structure of the liturgy.

The charismatic renewal requires the conciliar renewal for its proper ecclesial context, and the conciliar renewal needs charismatic renewal for its full transforming power. In the renewal of the full honoring of Mary there is a coming together of the Holy Spirit's renewing work in the reception of Scripture in the church, in the renewal of the liturgy, and in the new evangelization, all suffused with the new life of the Spirit, that is the hallmark of charismatic renewal. The inadequate patterns can only be corrected when CCR understands itself wholly in the context of the ecclesial renewal mandated by Vatican Two, and by the clear recognition within CCR that this grace came to the Catholic Church through the Pentecostals, and that it is inherently ecumenical.

It may be appropriate to conclude this chapter with a short story. At one of the first meetings of the TJCII international committee, there had been some mention of Mary and the Scriptures. Suddenly, one of the messianic Jewish brothers cried out in a loud voice, "Man, we've been robbed." He sensed in his guts that Israel had been deprived of one of her greatest daughters, and that in some way the Jewish Mary or Miriam had been stolen by the church, that had turned its back on the Jews and turned her into a *goy*.

12

A Deeper Significance to Baptism in the Spirit

THE INTERNATIONAL CCR HAS in recent times been led to focus again on the foundational grace of baptism in the Holy Spirit, with ICCRS publishing a document on this theme prepared by its doctrinal commission. This document acknowledges that when CCR began, "Baptism in the Holy Spirit had already been experienced within the Pentecostal movement for sixty years and within historic Protestant communions for seven to ten years."[1] For a full understanding of this work of the Holy Spirit, it is important to examine its history, and how this charismatic grace was understood from its beginnings.

From its origins the Pentecostal movement proclaimed the soon coming of the Lord in glory. Its central feature—baptism in the Holy Spirit—was experienced as heralding the times of the end. Baptism in the Holy Spirit unleashed an intense longing for the coming of the Lord Jesus in glory. This hope especially marked the Azusa Street revival where the key slogans were "Pentecost Has Come," and "He is coming soon." The outside world, insofar as it was aware of these Pentecostal beginnings—which was not very much—focused on the phenomenon of speaking in tongues. The Pentecostals were focused on the Lord and his coming. In his detailed account of Pentecostal origins, D. William Faupel, a scholar of early Pentecostalism, has written: "The second coming of Jesus was the central concern of the initial Pentecostal message."[2]

1. ICCRS, *Baptism*, 8.
2. Faupel, *Everlasting Gospel*, 20.

Four designations were quickly given to this revival: Full Gospel, Latter Rain, Apostolic Faith, and Pentecostal. The first three in particular had an eschatological emphasis. The Full Gospel that the Pentecostals proclaimed included the second coming as essential to the full message of Jesus Christ. The Latter Rain image took up the patterns of rainfall in the Holy Land, the spring and the autumn rains, understanding the Pentecostal revival as the latter rain restoring the intensity of Holy Spirit outpouring that had characterized the beginnings of the church at Pentecost. Latter Rain implied that the end was fast approaching. Apostolic Faith meant the restoration both of apostolic teaching (again with a focus on the coming of the Lord), and of apostolic power to win the world for Jesus. Here we find the strong missionary impulse that was so marked at Azusa Street, and in the early years of the Pentecostal movement. The urgency of the missionary task was linked to the soon coming of the Lord: the full gospel of full salvation must be proclaimed to all peoples before the Lord comes. A prophetic word at Azusa Street declared: "Awake! Awake! There is but time to dress and be ready, for the cry will soon go forth. The Bridegroom cometh."[3]

Some Pentecostals emphasized their focus on Jesus by speaking of the foursquare gospel, that is: Jesus saves, Jesus heals, Jesus baptizes with the Holy Spirit, and Jesus is coming soon. Notice that this fourfold summary is all in the present tense: Jesus acts, he acts now, and he acts in these ways. The order suggests that Jesus baptizing with Holy Spirit leads directly to Jesus coming in glory.

The initial Pentecostal message about the imminence of the Lord's coming emphasized the wonder of the coming glory, of which baptism in the Spirit was a foretaste, the urgency of the missionary proclamation, and the importance of holiness and obedience, so as to be overcomers on the day of judgment. The focus was not at first on detailed scenarios for the unfolding of the last days. But, as we shall see, the concept of "baptizing with Spirit" in the New Testament is strongly eschatological, which has helped the Pentecostal movement to retain an awareness of the Holy Spirit's role in preparing the church for the second coming.

With the spread of Pentecostal blessing to the historic churches in the charismatic movement, there is also evidence of an awakened hope for the second coming of the Lord. But it has not been right at the center as it

---

3. This headline appeared on the front page of the Azusa Street newsletter *The Apostolic Faith*, Oct. 1906. See also Corum, *Like as of Fire*, for compilation of the Azusa Street papers.

was in the Pentecostal origins. With the Pentecostals, the "blessed hope" of the Lord's coming was initially a driving motivational force for the whole movement. With the charismatic movement, the lordship of Jesus was at the center of the renewing work of the Holy Spirit, but it was his present lordship that was central, with less attention to his future lordship in the coming kingdom. Saying that Jesus baptizes with Holy Spirit affirms his active lordship through his disciples, demonstrated in tangible acts of power: saving, healing, casting out evil spirits, preaching the gospel. These signs may have been less dramatic among the charismatics than among the Pentecostals, but they have not been any less real. However, it is not true that the hope for the coming of the Lord has not been present. Numerous renewal songs and choruses testify to this hope: for example, the ever-popular "Bread of Life" song based on John 6, that came from the Word of God community in Ann Arbor, which has as refrain: "And I will raise him up, and I will raise him up, and I will raise him up on the last day." There are CCR groups and communities that have chosen the name Maranatha. Nonetheless, it remains true that the eschatological hope has not been as prominent in CCR, even in the origins, as it was with the Pentecostals.

The Biblical Witness

The phrase "baptism in the Spirit" does not occur in the New Testament in noun form. What we do find is the verb form, "baptize in/with Holy Spirit," generally without the definite article. There are no occasions where the phrase is used in a descriptive context, as occurs with the references to baptism as a rite of initiation (see Acts 2:41; 8:12–13, 38; 9:18; 10:48; 16:15, 33; 18:8; 19:5). In fact, whenever there is mention of being "baptized in Spirit," the occurrence is in a prophetic context. It belongs to the nature of the prophetic to be eschatological, sometimes more explicitly, at other times more implicitly. The first mentions of the phrase are very explicitly eschatological, that is in Matthew 3 and Luke 3. Here John says of the one who is to come, "He will baptize you with the Holy Spirit and with fire" (Matt 3:11; Luke 3:16). John the Baptist follows in the line of the Old Testament prophets, announcing future blessing and future judgment. Fire is an image associated with purification, and with punishment. In this instance, there is no reason to separate being baptized with fire from being baptized with Holy Spirit. The judgment reference is explicit in the words of Jesus that follow in both accounts: "His winnowing fork is in his hand, and he will clear his threshing floor and gather his wheat into the granary, but the chaff he will burn with unquenchable fire" (Matt 3:12; Luke 3:17).[4]

In John's gospel we are told that John "bore witness," saying, "he who sent me to baptize with water said to me, 'He on whom you see the Spirit descend and remain, this is he who baptizes with the Holy Spirit'" (John 1:32–33). Here the sense is even more strongly that baptizing with Holy Spirit will characterize the ministry of Jesus, whom John recognizes as the Lamb of God. This is above all what Jesus has come to do.

The phrase "baptize with Holy Spirit" occurs twice in the Acts of the Apostles, both times in prophetic rather than descriptive passages. The first is in chapter 1, referring to the words of the risen Jesus to the eleven apostles: "And while staying with them he charged them not to depart from Jerusalem, but to wait for the promise of the Father, which, he said, 'you heard from me, for John baptized with water, but before many days you shall be baptized with the Holy Spirit'" (Acts 1:4–5). The second reference is in chapter 11, when Peter is reporting to the community in Jerusalem about the coming of the Holy Spirit upon the centurion Cornelius and his household: "As I began to speak, the Holy Spirit fell on them just as on us at the beginning. And I remembered the word of the Lord, how he said, 'John baptized with water, but you shall be baptized with the Holy Spirit'" (Acts 11:15–16). So there are only two occasions or events where there are indications that people were baptized with the Holy Spirit. The first is the day of Pentecost, taking place "not many days after" the promise of Jesus, and that Peter later identifies as a day of fulfillment of this word. The second is what is sometimes called "the Gentile Pentecost" in Caesarea, described in chapter 10, and that Peter identifies as a parallel occurrence to the Jewish Pentecost in Jerusalem, described in chapter 2. In both cases, we find not a simple description, but a declaration of prophetic fulfillment. The phrase "baptize with Holy Spirit" is truly biblical, but it is essentially prophetic. The statement is a declaration about the ministry of the risen and ascended Jesus. It is an all-encompassing description of the deepest effects of the invasive power of God in and through Jesus. The plural "you" invokes a strongly corporate character. The two occasions of when this promise is said to be fulfilled are significant corporate occasions; they are both connected with the birth of the church.

We should notice that when the apostle Peter explains the extraordinary events on the day of Pentecost described in Acts 2, he presents them

---

4. In Mark there is reference just to "he [who] will baptize with Holy Spirit" (1:8), without any reference to fire.

as a fulfillment of the prophecy of Joel, that "in the last days . . . I will pour out my Spirit upon all flesh, and your sons and your daughters shall prophesy, and your young men shall see visions, and your old men shall dream dreams; yea, and on my menservants and my maidservants in those days I will pour out my Spirit; and they shall prophecy" (Joel 2:28–29). But it is significant that Peter does not stop his citation at this point, but continues with three more verses that are full of apocalyptic imagery. For example, "The sun shall be turned into darkness and the moon into blood, before the day of the Lord comes, the great and manifest day" (Acts 2:20, citing Joel 2:31). The clear implication is that the work of Jesus baptizing with Spirit and with fire, which is manifested on the day of Pentecost, will be totally fulfilled on the day of the Lord with the resurrection of the just to everlasting life, and the definitive separation of the wheat from the chaff.

Sometimes 1 Cor 12:13 is cited as another reference for baptism in the Spirit: "For by one Spirit we were all baptized into one body . . . and all were made to drink of one Spirit." This passage is best understood as a teaching about what was later called the sacrament or ordinance of baptism referring to the ritual act of being immersed in water. In other words, it is a reference to the role of the Holy Spirit in Christian initiation, and belongs to a genre that is quite different to the prophetic utterances of John the Baptist.

The Contemporary Application

If this is an authentic interpretation of the biblical witness to baptism in the Spirit, then we should look for the meaning of the contemporary outpouring of the Spirit first in relation to the eschatological hope. I suggest that when the first Pentecostals spoke of the outpouring of the Spirit at Azusa Street as baptism in the Spirit, they were not doing biblical exegesis. They were doing what the apostle Peter did on the day of Pentecost: they were speaking prophetically. Just as Peter cited the prophecy of Joel and told the assembled crowd, "this is what was spoken by the prophet Joel" (Acts 2:16), so the first Pentecostals were taking the biblical promises that Jesus will baptize with Holy Spirit, and saying, "This is that," of which John the Baptist spoke and that the Lord Jesus himself promised. Because those promises received a fulfillment at Pentecost, they said of the contemporary outpouring, "This is Pentecost."[5]

5. For example, the Azusa Street bulletin *Apostolic Faith* had such headlines as "Pentecost has Come" (Sept. 1906), "Pentecost with Signs Following" (Dec. 1906), and "Pentecost Both Sides the Ocean" (Feb.–Mar. 1907).

Just as Peter's citation of Joel included the description of apocalyptic shaking, so the first Pentecostals understood that this outpouring of the Spirit belongs to the preparation for the climax of history and the Lord's coming in glory. This conviction was reflected in titles of Pentecostal magazines, such as *The Bridegroom's Messenger, The Bridal Call, The Latter Rain Evangel,* and *The Midnight Cry.* The strong eschatological orientation of the biblical language of baptizing with Holy Spirit indicates that the deeper meaning of this contemporary outpouring lies in its being God's empowering and equipping of the whole church for the trials and triumphs of the final hour. The implications of Peter's citation of Joel in Acts 2 need to expand our understanding of being baptized in Holy Spirit. That is to say, being baptized in the Spirit now prepares Christians for the final and overwhelming Spirit-baptism on the last day, when their glorified and resurrected bodies will be totally penetrated and radiated by the Holy Spirit. The final chapter will look more specifically at the ecumenical significance of the Pentecostal and charismatic movements in the light of the eschatological hope.

How the Holy Spirit's Purpose was Frustrated

In the Pentecostal Movement

It seems that the heart of God's purpose in this Pentecostal awakening became sidelined by two different factors that deflected attention from the Holy Spirit's work of preparation. I will look at these influences in turn: first, the distraction from pre-millennial dispensationalism with the rise of fundamentalism; second, the distraction through arguments concerning the order of experienced blessings, and the issue of speaking in tongues as the "initial evidence" for baptism in the Spirit.

First, the milieux in which the Pentecostal revival broke out were affected by new currents in Evangelical circles, in particular two interlocking influences: (1) the pre-millennial dispensationalism associated with J. N. Darby and the Brethren movement, widely disseminated through the footnotes of the Scofield Reference Bible, published in 1909; and (2) the Evangelical rejection of Darwinian evolution, which was at the heart of a fight against the new biblical criticism that was bringing evolutionary theories of historical development into the interpretation of the Scriptures. The first factor produced a focus on detailed timetables and sequences of events for the end times (rapture, great tribulation, millennial reign). The second gave rise to a fundamentalism, which in practice eliminated the dimension of mystery, and sharply reduced the role of the Holy Spirit in Christian life, in exegesis, and in preaching. As a consequence of these conservative Evangelical influences, the living hope for the Lord's coming was distorted by the false idea that prophecy is "history written beforehand," and was undermined by the temptation to claim "insider knowledge" of the future. What mattered most was the correct understanding of the events to come, described as "rightly dividing the Word." The focus was shifted from the living hope formed by the Holy Spirit within the body of Christ to issues of knowledge and prophetic interpretation.

Secondly, many of the first Pentecostals came from currents impacted by the Holiness movement, whether in its moderate form (associated with the Keswick conventions), or its more radical forms that were issuing in new Holiness denominations in the United States.[6] These milieux had a focus on sanctification as a work of the Holy Spirit to be experienced, whether in a process (moderate view), or in a one-time identifiable experience (radical view). The former often had a background in Reformed theology, while the latter had largely developed from Wesleyan roots. But both experienced and understood the Pentecostal baptism in the Spirit as a new and identifiable once-and-for-all experience. For those from a Reformed background, sanctification was the outworking of regeneration-conversion, and so for them baptism in the Spirit was understood as a second-stage experience. For those from a Wesleyan background, already affirming sanctification as a second experience, the Pentecostal baptism in the Spirit became a third experiential stage in Christian discipleship. These differences drew discussion on baptism in the Spirit away from its end-times context into questions of the proper order in Christian experience. The issue of how you can know for certain that you have received this baptism further complicated the debates. The majority of Pentecostals opted for speaking in tongues as the necessary "initial evidence" of Spirit-baptism. If you have once spoken in tongues, then you have been baptized in the Spirit; if you haven't, then you have not received.[7] As a result, Pentecostal literature has given disproportionate space to the issue of

6. For example, the Church of the Nazarene, and the Church of God Anderson, Indiana.

7. Most Pentecostals thus distinguished an initial speaking in tongues as the evidence of Spirit-baptism from the gift of speaking in tongues that is an ongoing endowment. This distinction was never received within the charismatic movement.

"initial evidence," which then easily becomes a distraction from the fundamental significance of baptism in the Spirit.

Another aspect of distancing from the initial outpouring of the Spirit
was a shift from a communal setting to almost entirely individualistic application. Although the Pentecostals always insisted that each individual
receive "his/her Pentecost," there was at Azusa Street a strong sense of
something shared and communal. But as the Pentecostal revival spread in
the North American culture that was becoming increasingly individualistic and oriented to personal fulfillment, the trend increased to understand
baptism in the Spirit simply as an individual blessing, though occurring on
a large scale. These trends were however less strong in the African American and the Hispanic communities, where the Pentecostal movement was
soon to make an impact. But these subcultures were not those that shaped
the theological debate that has dominated Pentecostal discourse. The less-
ening sense of a gift for the body of Christ, and the greater focus on the individual Christian, also weakened the eschatological hope. For the hope for
the whole body of Christ is the Lord's coming in glory, the resurrection of
the dead, and the establishment of the Lord's reign. The hope of individual
Christians is personal salvation, and going to heaven when they die.

In the Charismatic Movement

As I have noted, the heightened awareness and anticipation of the Lord's
coming in glory was less marked in the origins of the charismatic movement than in the Pentecostal. But here too the focus of attention was rather
quickly drawn away from its significance within Christian history to issues
concerning Christian initiation.

Charismatics in an Evangelical context tended to accept the "two-
stage" Pentecostal teaching about baptism in the Spirit as a post-conversion
reception of the Spirit, while being less insistent than the Pentecostals on
speaking in tongues as the necessary initial evidence. Charismatics with a
sacramental background, and most obviously the Catholics, focused on the
relationship between baptism in the Spirit and the sacraments of initiation,
particularly of baptism. Just as most Pentecostals upheld baptism in the
Spirit as a distinctive second blessing, so most sacramental charismatics
interpreted baptism in the Spirit as an actualization or entry into conscious
experience of the graces objectively conferred in sacramental baptism. Although the historic churches, particularly those of a liturgical-sacramental

character, embody at their heart the corporate character of Christian faith, their members have also been much affected by the individualist consumerist culture pervading the modern Western world. So while charismatic Catholics typically think of baptism in the Spirit first as a personal blessing, they generally understand that this work of the Spirit is a gift for the church. Nonetheless along with the pervasive individualism, the focus on grounding baptism in the Spirit in the sacraments of initiation has deflected attention away from its fundamental meaning at this point in Christian history.

However, the deepest reasons for this weaker eschatological orientation in the charismatic movement flow directly from two related factors: first, the distancing of the church from the Jewish roots; and second, the "marriage" of church and empire from the time of Constantine. The empire-church links were so strong that the unity of the church and the unity of the empire were seen as two facets of the same unity.[8] Inevitably this bonding of church and empire tended to favor a theological equation between the church and the kingdom of God. As the Roman Empire officially embraced Christianity in the fourth century, the church turned away from the concept of a future millennial reign of Christ. The millennium was then understood to have begun with the conquest of paganism and the end of persecution. It seems to have been no accident that these changes took place just as the church distanced herself from the Jewish people and their feasts. In consequence the movements preaching preparation for the coming of the Lord in glory typically arose on the fringes of the established church or outside its communion. This consequence of church-empire cohabitation continued, even as the political empire fragmented through the formation of state or national churches, regulated by concordat for churches in communion with Rome, and by state law for the established Protestant churches. A living eschatology was hardly possible in such historical conditions, for established churches are inherently allergic to socially destabilizing movements!

However, it is worth noting that at the Second Vatican Council the Catholic Church decisively asserted the independence of the church from all forms of political power and government. Though this separation was not eschatologically motivated, it has in fact freed the Catholic Church to

---

8. This thinking was clearly demonstrated when the empire in the West collapsed, and the pope consecrated an emperor (Charlemagne) in the West, an action that the Eastern church under Constantinople regarded as schismatic, as implying the creation of a second church.

embrace its eschatological destiny, a consequence that has not so far greatly penetrated into Catholic consciousness.[9]

Another major obstacle to Catholics acquiring a living eschatology has been a mistaken way of opposing the Evangelical and the sacramental. In this wrong way of thinking, Catholics think that God does not act directly on the believer, but only acts through priests and rites. So rather than experiencing God, Catholics experience liturgy and religious practices that communicate the grace of God. In this way of thinking Catholics easily dismiss as heretical and sectarian the Evangelical conviction that God acts directly on the human spirit without priestly liturgical mediation. But this attitude represents a wrong way of understanding liturgy, sacraments, and the ordained ministry. The theological difference between the Evangelical and the Catholic is not between direct experience of the Lord (Evangelical-charismatic), and mediated grace without experience (Catholic-sacramental). The teaching of John Paul II makes clear that the Catholic Church needs both the institutional (Word of God, liturgy and sacraments, magisterium) and the charismatic (unpredictable interventions of the sovereign Lord). Without the charismatic dimension, there is a real danger that the institutional (in particular the sacramental) is not perceived and lived as the activity of Jesus, and that sacramental observance seems to replace the experience and knowledge of Christ. For the Catholic the sacramental signs in Catholic liturgy signify the total work of God right up to the final completion with the coming of Jesus and the resurrection of the body. Through the sacramental sign, we receive and can experience the grace of God, because in the liturgy it is Jesus who is acting through his ministers. But while the sacramental sign symbolizes the total work of salvation, what we experience and receive now is a foretaste, a sample of the glory that is to come. Each time that we participate in the liturgy, we advance a step closer to the final glory. The apostle Paul speaks of us having "the first fruits of the Spirit," through which we "groan inwardly as we wait for adoption as sons, the redemption of our bodies" (Rom 8:23). In Ephesians, we read of those who have heard the gospel of salvation with faith described as "sealed with the Holy Spirit of promise, which is the guarantee of our inheritance until we acquire possession of it" (Eph 1:13–14).[10]

9. The recovery of such an eschatological vision was begun rather cautiously in *LG* chap. 7, and was then carried a little further in the *CCC* (see 675–77).

10. In this passage, I have changed the RSV translation "the promised Holy Spirit" to reflect the genitive in the Greek text. The "promised Holy Spirit" can just mean the Holy Spirit promised in the past; that is, in the Old Testament prophets, rather than the Holy Spirit, who was and still remains the Spirit of promise.

The Eschatological Hope and the Scriptures

A further reason for a weaker hope for the coming of the Lord among Catholics is often their poor knowledge of the Bible. This weakness extends to priests, despite more attention being given to biblical studies since the Second Vatican Council. At the Roman synod of bishops on the Word of God in 2008, several bishops attributed the weakness of much Catholic preaching to poor knowledge of the Scriptures.

What CCR has contributed to the Catholic Church is a great thirst for the Scriptures among the Catholics baptized in the Spirit. Through the Spirit they have been given an interior resonance or affinity with the written Word. They become conscious of having within them the same Spirit that authored and inspired the written Word of God. The council document on divine revelation has taught: "Sacred Scripture must be read and interpreted in the light of the same Spirit by whom it was written."[11] So Catholics in the renewal typically want to know the Scriptures, and they want to be taught. Perhaps the biggest problem is a lack of quality teaching. For Catholics truly to take hold of the "blessed hope" of the Lord's coming in glory, they need regular teaching accompanied by constant feeding on the Word of God. With regular reading of the Scriptures, the Holy Spirit will show the alert reader how the Scriptures are full of the promises of the Lord for the messianic kingdom, and for the coming of the Lord in glory.

The first principle of interpretation that the Second Vatican Council gives concerns the unity of the Bible. "Different as the books which comprise it may be, Scripture is a unity by reason of the unity of God's plan, of which Christ Jesus is the center and heart, open since his Passover."[12] The Scriptures unveil for us the one plan of God that has been revealed in his Son. But we can only see and grasp this unity through the Holy Spirit. The apostle Paul uses a special word for this one plan of God that we can only know through revelation: the word mystery, which he speaks of as "the mystery of Christ."

While the magisterium of pope and bishops acts as a protection against doctrinal deviation within the Catholic Church, there would appear to be less effective protection against bizarre and deviant currents in popular piety. There has certainly been an apocalyptic element in the messages being disseminated from the places where apparitions have occurred,

11. *DV* 12.
12. *CCC* 112.

in those approved by church authority, and probably more in those not yet approved, and those already disapproved. But this apocalyptic dimension has mostly comprised warnings of potentially imminent horrors and coming judgment. The apparitions of modern times can hardly be said to have awakened the eschatological hope, and a joyful longing for the coming of the Lord. The remedy for these weaknesses is a deeper rooting in the Scriptures, and the work of the risen Lord who baptizes with the Holy Spirit.

13

The Holy Spirit and the One Hope of Glory

THE ESCHATOLOGICAL "END-TIMES" SIGNIFICANCE of baptism in the Spirit as experienced in the Pentecostal and charismatic movements has been indicated in chapter 12. What remains to be considered is the connection between "the blessed hope" of the Lord's coming and the quest for Christian unity. The essential connection between eschatology and unity is summed up in the short biblical phrase "the one hope," that the apostle Paul includes in the list of what is unique in Ephesians 4:4–6: "There is one body and one Spirit, just as you were called to the *one hope* that belongs to your call, one Lord, one faith, one baptism, one God and Father of us all, who is above all and through all and in all." All Christians have this same call; to whatever church or tradition we belong. We are all called to the same hope: all Christians are "awaiting our blessed hope, the appearing of the glory of our great God and Savior Jesus Christ" (Titus 2:13). There is one hope, the hope for the coming of the one king, the hope for the one kingdom, whose fullness he will embody and establish.

This hope is a deepening and an expansion in the hope of Israel. The promises given to Israel are centered on a coming messianic age when the Messiah-Savior will establish righteousness on the earth, when all evil will be banished, and the fullness of covenant union between the chosen people and their God will be realized. When Paul, the apostle to the nations, arrives in Rome as a prisoner, he explains to the leaders of the Jewish community that "it is because of the hope of Israel that I am bound with this chain" (Acts 28:20). For Paul, the hope of the church is the hope of Israel transformed through Jesus, but it is still the hope of Israel. Thus, the *Catechism of the Catholic Church* in its section on the coming of the Lord can have as a sub heading, "The Glorious Advent of Christ, the Hope of Israel."[1]

The church's affirmation of the ongoing unrevoked covenant of the Lord with Israel means that God's promises to Israel remain fully in force, whatever interpretations Jews and Christians may have placed upon them. When Christians affirm these promises, then the key question for our eschatology becomes: "What difference has the first coming of the Messiah made to the hope of Israel?" It is wrong to say that all the promises to Israel have already been fulfilled in the incarnation, as though the hope of the church is substantially different from the hope of Israel. But there is not one hope in the Old Testament, and a different hope in the New Testament. The hope of the church is the hope of Israel transformed by the first coming of the Messiah, and by the gift of the indwelling Holy Spirit. We can sum up this transformation within the hope of Israel in this way:

1. In the New Testament, the identity of the Messiah is revealed, and his character and his mission made manifest. The Catholic Catechism teaches here: "God's People of the Old Covenant and the new People of God tend towards similar goals: expectation of the coming (or the return) of the Messiah. But one awaits the return of the Messiah who died and rose from the dead and is recognized as Lord and Son of God; the other awaits the coming of a Messiah, whose features remain hidden till the end of time."[2]

2. The gift of the Holy Spirit makes the hope of Israel a living hope within the heart of each believer. The Holy Spirit not only reveals the reality and the meaning of the resurrection of Jesus, but already indwells the Christian so that the divine life within grounds the hope for our future resurrection. It is the revelation of the resurrection, "each one in his own order: Christ the firstfruits, afterward those who are Christ's at his coming" (1 Cor 15:23), that is the distinctively new and transforming element in the hope of the church.[3] As St. Peter explains: "By his great mercy we have been born anew to a living hope through the resurrection of Jesus Christ from the dead, and to an inheritance

1. Heading above para. 673.

2. CCC 840.

3. Here the church is to be understood as renewed Israel, into which the Gentiles are ingrafted, not as a new entity separate from the Jewish people.

which is imperishable, undefiled, and unfading, kept in heaven for you" (1 Pet 1:3–4).

3. This transformation of Jesus in his humanity through his resurrection and ascension reveals God's purpose to glorify the whole material creation, and bring it to its full harmony and perfection. In our future resurrection from the dead, we shall receive a "spiritual body," as St. Paul writes: "It is sown a physical body, it is raised a spiritual body" (1 Cor 15:44). The hope of Israel as a people in this world for deliverance from all oppression will be realized by the glorification of redeemed humankind and of the whole creation, that "will be set free from its bondage to decay and obtain the glorious liberty of the children of God" (Rom 8:21). This glorification will not turn human beings into angels, but will fill all material reality with the one glory of Christ.

The Scandal of Christian Division

Much has been written about the scandal of Christian division. Our divisions have been denounced as a counter-witness to the truth of the gospel, literally as a *skandalon*, an obstacle to faith. So Jesus prays to the Father that his disciples may be one, as he and the Father are one, "so that the world may believe that thou hast sent me" (John 17:21). Our divisions have been castigated for demonstrating how little Christians love another, in direct contradiction of the Lord's words, "By this all men will know that you are my disciples, if you have love for one another" (John 13:35). But far fewer have deplored our divisions as a denial of the "one hope."

In fact, the one hope, the promise of the unity of the kingdom of God, manifests the deepest ground for the evil of divisions. For the other grounds of scandal show their full evil in their relationship to the one hope. The scandal of division hinders world evangelization because the divisions obscure the gospel of the kingdom, and ultimately make it unbelievable, for the gospel is "the message of reconciliation" (2 Cor 5:19). Our divisions show that we have not fully received the message we want to preach to others. The lack of love is most shaming because the kingdom will be the fullness of love, the complete sharing of Trinitarian communion in Christ. Our divisions are most scandalous because they demonstrate how unready the Christian churches are for the Lord's coming.

In the end we have to say that when our Christian life, personal and corporate, is not oriented toward the final consummation, then we have not properly understood what it is to be a Christian, what it is to be baptized, what it is to receive the Holy Spirit.

The Contribution of the Pentecostal-Charismatic Renewal

What then is the contribution of the charismatic renewal to Christian awareness and appropriation of "the blessed hope, the appearing of the glory of our great God and Savior Jesus Christ" (Titus 2:13)? It can be summed up in terms of content or clearer vision, in terms of inner longing and orientation, and in terms of foretaste and anticipation.

Content or Clearer Vision

The Holy Spirit reveals the person and mission of Jesus, above all as we hear and read the Scriptures. The Spirit reveals to each Christian the Jesus who has come, and the Lord who will come in glory. Jesus says of the Spirit: "He will take what is mine and declare it to you" (John 16:15), and, as Jesus said, "he will declare to you the things that are to come" (John 16:13). This knowledge of Jesus is not about when he will come, for he said explicitly, "But of that day and hour no one knows, not even the angels of heaven, nor the Son, but the Father only" (Matt 24:36). It is an inner certainty that he will come, and that he will come in glory. His coming will be "the time for establishing all that God spoke by the mouth of his holy prophets from of old" (Acts 3:21). As mentioned, its heart will be the resurrection of the dead, and the liberation of all creation from its bondage to decay. As Paul tells the Romans, "we rejoice in our hope of sharing the glory of God" (Rom 5:2). This hope "does not disappoint us, because God's love has been poured into our hearts through the Holy Spirit which has been given to us" (Rom 5:5).

Inner Longing and Orientation

The phrase, "the blessed hope," speaks of something the Holy Spirit places within us. It is not only more knowledge, but also deep desire. The apostle Paul described this inner hope in terms of a deep longing: "Here indeed we groan, and long to put on our heavenly dwelling, so that by putting it on we may not be found naked" (2 Cor 5:2–3). This longing is expressed in a different way in 2 Timothy 4: "Henceforth there is laid up for me the crown of righteousness, which the Lord, the righteous judge, will award to me on that Day, and not only to me but also to all those who have loved his appearing" (2 Tim 4:8).[4] This longing and groaning is itself prayer for the fulfillment, a prayer that itself hastens the day of completion (see 2 Pet 3:12).

Foretaste and Anticipation

The longing has a sure foundation in the gift of the Holy Spirit. As Paul says in Romans 8:23, the Spirit is given to the Christian as "first fruits," so that "we groan inwardly as we wait for our adoption as sons, the redemption of our bodies." This taste of the first-fruits contains within it the desire to enjoy the fullness of the Spirit in the coming kingdom. So the foretaste, the inner longing, and the content all come together. It is this taste of new life within, with new awareness, new capacities, new interests, and new desires that produces the longing for the fullness to come. The Holy Spirit, who gives us a taste now of the beauty and truth of Jesus, gives us the longing for the complete union with Jesus and all his saints.

The Role of the Liturgy

Up to this point, what has been said of the "blessed hope" may seem to have focused on the individual Christian. However, as was emphasized in chapter 12, the hope of the church is a corporate hope, it is the hope for the one kingdom to come. Without a living liturgy in which this hope is proclaimed and celebrated, we are unlikely to experience the blessed hope as the hope of the church. Pope Benedict XVI has insisted repeatedly that the Scriptures and the liturgy are closely connected. The liturgy is the worship of the community that feeds on the Scriptures, as the church's liturgy is largely comprised of the Scriptures and the use of biblical symbols and images.

Because the Scriptures present the history of salvation, with its fulcrum in the first coming of Jesus, a history that will reach its fulfillment with the Lord's coming in glory, the liturgy has this fundamental orientation to the

4. Some translations have "longed for his appearing," but the Greek text has *egapekosi* (i.e., loved, which is a way of emphasizing a deep longing of the heart).

future coming of the Lord. So the *Catechism of the Catholic Church* states: "The church celebrates the mystery of her Lord 'until he comes,' when God will be 'everything to everyone.' Since the apostolic age the liturgy has been drawn towards its goal by the Spirit's groaning in the church: *Marana tha!*"[5] This hope of the church is expressed in two of the three acclamations introduced into the eucharistic prayer of the Roman rite after the consecration.[6] But it is during the Our Father that follows the eucharistic prayer that the gathered church prays most intensely for the Lord's coming. It is the appropriate moment for all to raise their arms, and together consciously to beg the Lord to come.[7] The Catholic Catechism teaches explicitly: "In the eucharist, the Lord's Prayer also reveals the eschatological character of its petitions. It is the proper prayer of 'the end-time,' the time of salvation that began with the outpouring of the Holy Spirit, and will be fulfilled with the Lord's return."[8]

The Scripture and the liturgy operate hand in hand to shape and move the church towards the coming king and his kingdom. Light from the Word is essential—not just light for the individual, but light for the church community—but this has to be expressed in worship, which is the declaration of our stance before God. This is why the real nature of the church is shown and revealed in the liturgical assembly, when we gather to hear the Word of God, and to celebrate the mighty acts of God in praise and liturgical action.[9] The renewal of the liturgy will only be achieving its full goal when whole congregations cry "Come" with full heart and voice. As this happens the hope of the church will be restored.

5. *CCC* 1130.

6. The first is, "We proclaim your death, O Lord, and profess your resurrection until you come again." And the second, "When we eat this bread and drink this cup, we proclaim your death, O Lord, until you come again."

7. The widespread practice of joining hands for the Our Father only acquires its full meaning when the people are consciously praying together for the coming of the Lord. Doing it simply as a celebration of togetherness can turn attention away to ourselves.

8. *CCC* 2771. The Catechism goes on in its commentary on "Thy Kingdom Come" to say, "This petition is 'Marana tha', the cry of the Spirit and the Bride: 'Come, Lord Jesus.'" para. 2817.

9. "The principal manifestation of church consists in the full, active participation of all God's holy people in the same liturgical celebrations, especially in the same eucharist, in one prayer, at one altar, at which the bishop presides, surrounded by his college of priests and by his ministers." *SC* 41.

The Gift of an Ecumenical Renewal

If the work of the Holy Spirit is to prepare the church for the coming of the Lord, and to gather all into unity in and under Jesus Christ, then the situation of division in which it is impossible for separated Christian communities to celebrate a totally shared liturgy is almost blasphemous. How can we be prepared for our common destiny in one kingdom under one Lord when we do not hear the Word of God together, and we do not together celebrate the memorial of the Lord? The current Catholic criteria for the possibility of admitting other Christians to eucharistic communion always include belief in the real presence of the Lord in the sacrament. The church remembers and the church hopes. So we when we remember the Last Supper and the words of Jesus concerning his body and his blood, we need to remember that his coming in the eucharist anticipates his coming in glory. So we need to ask: is it not an important criterion for eucharistic communion whether there is present a clear belief in and longing for the coming of the Lord, who is making himself present as foretaste and anticipation?

The unique gift of the renewal for unity is that here the Lord has been pouring out the same grace, the same life, the same gifts on Christians from all churches and traditions. Especially in the revelation of Jesus as the living Lord, and in the release of love and adoration for the Lord from the heart, Christians from all kinds of backgrounds have been enabled to worship and to praise the Lord together. They are also able to proclaim together their common destiny as the Holy Spirit restores to Christian hearts the cry "Marana tha," "Come, Lord Jesus" (1 Cor 16:22; Rev 22:20). The extraordinary grace of this common worship is powerfully symbolized in the gift of tongues, when the spontaneous singing in the Spirit of disparate peoples produces a harmony that no human conductor has fashioned. Since those who speak in a tongue utter "mysteries in the Spirit" (1 Cor 14:2), this joint singing in tongues is a longing for the glory to be revealed.

As mentioned in earlier chapters, some Christians baptized in the Spirit were led to form ecumenical communities, almost all with Catholic majorities. They were convinced that the shared grace they experienced could and should be made the foundation for shared lives together in community. However, it seems that these communities have not led the way in understanding the eschatological character of baptism in the Spirit, and the importance of the one shared hope for Christian unity. This is most likely to happen as they awaken to the ongoing role of Israel in the mystery of Christ.

The One Goal Purifies and Brings into One

The blessed hope of the coming of the Lord and his kingdom makes another essential contribution to the work for Christian unity. As the Holy Spirit opens our eyes to the day of the Lord, to the final judgment, to the coming of Jesus in glory, there is revealed the horizon against which all else is to be understood and assessed.[10] The word in 1 John that "everyone who thus hopes in him purifies himself as he is pure" (1 John 3:3), also has application to the faith of communities and whole churches. It is vision of the final goal that reveals the distortion that happens when anything less than the final goal is made final or absolute. The divisions of church history have absolutized the differences. Turning created and intermediate goals into absolutes distorts Christian faith. The "blessed hope" de-absolutizes and places everything else in relation to the final goal of the kingdom of God. For this reason, the hope is inherently purifying.

The completion of all things requires that the church as the body of Christ embodies the full witness of the Holy Spirit to Jesus, so that the distinctive witness of every church and tradition finds its place in the one body. The Lord is coming for his bride. Without the work of the Holy Spirit in every tradition, the bride is not prepared. She is only half clothed. In the book of Revelation, we are told of the bride: "It was granted her to be clothed with fine linen, bright and pure—for the fine linen is the righteous deeds of the saints" (Rev 19:8). We can say that the adornment of the bride includes the full work of the Spirit: in theological heritage, in worship, in lived communion, and above all in the lives of the martyrs and the most holy witnesses to Jesus. The Pentecostal-charismatic outpouring of the Spirit has to be important for this preparation, precisely because it is awakening living faith and hope across almost the whole Christian spectrum.

As a specific work of God in our day the Pentecostal charismatic renewal highlights the sovereign revivifying work of the Holy Spirit that extends way beyond all organized forms of renewal. As unpredictable charismatic works of the Lord, the Pentecostal and charismatic movements in their various expressions prepare the whole body of Christ in a particular way for the greatest and most unpredictable charismatic event of all, the coming of the Lord in glory, and the resurrection of the dead.

---

10. The day of the Lord is also called in the New Testament, "the day of our Lord Jesus Christ" (1 Cor 1:8), "the day of the Lord Jesus" (2 Cor 1:14), "the day of Jesus Christ" (Phil 1:6), "the day of Christ" (Phil 2:16), "the day of the Lord" (1 Thess 5:2; 2 Thess 2:2), "the day of God" (2 Pet 3:12), or simply "that day" (1 Thess 5:4; 2 Tim 1:12; 4:8).

Baptism in the Spirit as the Lord's Preparation

A deeper reflection on the biblical usage of the language of baptizing with Holy Spirit, and a deeper analysis of the origins of the Pentecostal movement, both point to the twentieth-century outpouring of the Holy Spirit as a God-given preparation for the final salvation to come with the coming of the Lord Jesus in glory and the resurrection of the just.[11] Such an understanding is confirmed by the ecumenical character of this outpouring, and its extension to the Jewish people in much of the messianic Jewish movement.

Does this mean that the second coming of the Lord is imminent? Maybe, but not necessarily. In the Lord's eyes, the coming in glory for which he longs is always imminent. It has been so since his first coming: "He who testifies to these things says, 'Surely, I am coming soon'" (Rev 22:20). It is interesting that the Catholic Catechism uses here the language of "suspension": "The glorious Messiah's coming is suspended at every moment of history until . . ."[12] Jesus is poised to come until the conditions are fulfilled, "until his recognition by 'all Israel.'"[13]

To summarize, we can say that in the whole renewal movement, Jesus is revealing the sovereign character of his Lordship. Jesus is the one who baptizes with Holy Spirit (John 1:33), and he does so as the sovereign Lord and Messiah, who has been raised to the right hand of the Father in the fullness of his humanity. This is the reason why baptism in the Spirit belongs to the charismatic dimension of the church—and indeed reveals in a particularly clear way the character of the charismatic as unforeseeable sovereign activity of the risen Lord.

It seems wholly appropriate that Almighty God should prepare for the glorious coming of his Son by a sovereign charismatic outpouring of his love, mercy, and power. The appropriateness is better evident because the coming of the Lord in glory will be the ultimate charismatic event. Jesus himself emphasized that no one knows the day nor the hour, only the Father: "For as the lightning comes from the east and shines as far as the west, so will be the coming of the Son of man" (Matt 24:27). The church is summoned to be ready: "Therefore you also must be ready; for the Son of man is coming at an hour you do not expect" (Matt 24:44).

11. Mention is not made here to the resurrection of the unrighteous (see John 5:29), as that can hardly be described as salvation.

12. CCC 674.

13. Ibid.

Charismatic Renewal and Christian Unity

A statement of European Catholic Leaders
in CCR from Disentis, Switzerland

June 15–17, 1989[1]

1. The heart of the charismatic renewal is the grace of what is variously known as "baptism in the Spirit, effusion de l'Esprit, Geistausgiessung." This faith event is a living experience of the lordship of Jesus Christ, giving the Christian an awareness of the presence and action of the Holy Spirit and a knowledge of being a beloved son or daughter of the Father.

2. This grace of the Spirit brings new life to all aspects of Christian faith and practice, producing new vitality and power in praise, evangelism, and service. Thus the charismatic renewal is not merely a grace for some aspect of the Christian life, such as evangelism or prayer, but is a multi-faceted current of renewal for the revitalization of the whole body of Christ.

3. The basic gift of God in charismatic renewal is the same across all the different Christian Churches and groupings touched in this movement of the Spirit. Its inter-church roots and origins have given birth to deep ecumenical relationships within the renewal, universally stimulating hopes for the realization of that unity for which all Christians pray.

---

1. As a European document, the text is quoted in British English.

4. The Catholic understanding of Christian faith excludes any separation between Jesus and the Church. Experience of the Lord is always related to the ecclesial community and its articulation is always shaped by its context within the Church. Catholic Christians therefore see the grace of charismatic renewal as inseparably a grace for each Church and a grace for the unity of the one Church of Christ.

5. This pentecostal experience enables ordinary believers to appreciate the teaching of Vatican II concerning the *hierarchy of truths*, which "vary in their relationship to the foundation of the Christian faith."[2] It demonstrates the role of the Holy Spirit in revealing within believers this foundation of the Christian faith: the majesty of Jesus as the eternal Son of the Father, established in his crucified and glorified humanity as Saviour of all, victor over the works of Satan, and head of the new creation.

6. This charismatic experience does not eliminate the distinctive elements of particular Christian traditions. Rather the Holy Spirit reveals them in their proper context as they relate to the great mystery centred on Christ. With this knowledge of the centre, the distinctives can come to be cherished, celebrated, and practiced in ways that diminish their unacceptability or ambiguity in the eyes of Christians from other Church traditions.

7. This illumination by the Spirit of the core of Christian faith within believers should not lead charismatic Christians away from their Church traditions, but should lead them to experience more deeply what it is to be at the spiritual center of their own Church tradition. The ecumenical dimension of the charismatic renewal should not reduce Church commitment and loyalty, but should purify them.

8. As a result of their pentecostal experience, many charismatic Christians of different Churches know a new level of unity with each other in the Spirit. However, this unity in the Spirit is to be understood not as a spiritual unity over and against the Churches, but as part of the Spirit's dynamic to bring entire separate communions into unity with each other. This shared unity in the Spirit is itself incomplete and of its inner nature calls for full sacramental and institutional embodiment.

---

2. *UR* 11.

9. As an unexpected work of the Holy Spirit, the charismatic renewal necessarily makes challenges and poses theological questions that cannot be immediately resolved. Theological reflection on all aspects of this outpouring of grace is essential, and requires an ecumenical component in accordance with its ecumenical character. This theological work needs to be pursued in a spirit of prayer, reverence, and discernment, and in full recognition of the ecclesial character of Christian theology as the science of faith.

Bibliography

Anon. "Retreats in Peru and Chile." *NC* (May 1972) 22–23.

Au, Connie. *Grassroots Unity in the Charismatic Renewal.* Eugene, OR: Wipf & Stock, 2011.

Benedict XVI. "Ecumenical Meeting." World Youth Day, Cologne, Germany, August 19, 2005. No pages. Online: http://www.vatican.va/holy_father/benedict_xvi/speeches/2005/august/documents/hf_ben-xvi_spe_20050819_ecumenical-meeting_en.html.

———. *Sacramentum Caritatis* (Post-synodal exhortation). London: Catholic Truth Society, 2007.

Bergoglio, Cardinal Jorge. Address to Conclave. No Pages. Online: http://en.radiovaticana.va/m_articolo.asp?c=677269.

Bittlinger, Arnold. *Gifts and Graces: A Commentary on 1 Corinthians 12–14.* Translated by Herbert Klassen. London: Hodder & Stoughton, 1973.

———. *Gifts and Ministries.* London: Hodder & Stoughton, 1974.

———, ed. *The Church is Charismatic.* Geneva: WCC, 1981.

Catholic Charismatic Renewal Service Committee. "Service Committee Issues Ecumenical Statement." *NC* (Jan 1974) 19–20.

Chan, Simon. "Mother-Church: Toward a Pentecostal Ecclesiology." *Pneuma* 22, no. 2 (2000) 177–208.

———. *Pentecostal Theology and the Christian Spiritual Tradition.* Sheffield: Sheffield Academic Press, 2000.

Clark, Stephen B. *Building Christian Communities: Strategy for Renewing the Church.* Notre Dame, IN: Ave Maria Press, 1975.

———. *Where Are We Headed?* Ann Arbor, MI: Charismatic Renewal Services, 1973.

The Code of Canon Law. London: Collins, 1983.

Commission for Religious Relations with the Jews. *Notes on the Correct Way to Present the Jews and Judaism.* In *Catholic Jewish Relations,* 31–49. London: Catholic Truth Society, 1999.

Corum, Fred T., comp. *Like as of Fire: A Reprint of the Old Azusa Street Papers.* Wilmington, MA: Corum, 1981.

Crowe, Terrence R. *Pentecostal Unity: Recurring Frustrations and Enduring Hopes.* Chicago, IL: Loyola University Press, 1993.

Doll, Jerry. "Colombia." *NC* (Feb 1973) 20–21.

Dombes, Groupe des. *For the Conversion of the Churches.* Geneva: WCC, 1993.

———. *Mary in the Plan of God and the Communion of Saints: Toward a Common Christian Understanding.* New York: Paulist, 2001.

Du Plessis, David, and Bob Slosser. *A Man Called Mr. Pentecost*. Plainfield, NJ: Logos, 1977.

Fabre, Laurent. "Le Renouveau charismatique: un témoignage." *Lumière et Vie* 125 (Nov–Dec 1975) 7–21.

Faupel, D. William. *The Everlasting Gospel: The Significance of Eschatology in the Development of Pentecostal Thought*. Sheffield: Sheffield Academic Press, 1996.

Fisher, E. J., and L. Klenicki. *Spiritual Pilgrimage: Pope John Paul II, Texts on Jews and Judaism 1979–1995*. New York: Crossroad, 1995.

Flannery, Austin, OP, ed. *Vatican Council II*. Constitutions, Decrees, Declarations. Northport, NY: Costello, 1996.

Flynn, Thomas. *The Charismatic Renewal and the Irish Experience*. London: Hodder & Stoughton, 1974.

Francis. Address to media representatives on March 16, 2013. No Pages. Online: www.vatican.va/holy_father/francesco/speeches/2013/march/documents/papa-francesco-20130316-rappresentanti-media_en.html.

———. Homily to College of Cardinals on March 15, 2013. No Pages. Online: www.vatican.va/holy_father/francesco/speeches/2013/march/documents/papa-francesco-20130315-cardinali_en.html.

Harper, Michael. *None Can Guess*. Plainfield, NJ: Logos, 1971.

———. *Three Sisters: A Provocative Look at Evangelicals, Charismatics and Catholic Charismatics and Their Relationship to One Another*. Carol Stream, IL: Tyndale, 1979.

Hocken, Peter. "Catholic Pentecostalism: Some Key Questions." *HJ* (1974) 131–43, 271–84.

———. *The Challenges of the Pentecostal Charismatic and Messianic Jewish Movements*. Farnham, UK: Ashgate, 2009.

———. "Charismatic Communities." In *The New International Dictionary of the Pentecostal and Charismatic Movements*, edited by Stanley M. Burgess and Eduard van der Maas, 473–76. Grand Rapids, MI: Zondervan, 2002.

———. "Charismatic Movement." In *The New International Dictionary of the Pentecostal and Charismatic Movements*, edited by Stanley M. Burgess and Eduard van der Maas, 477–519. Grand Rapids, MI: Zondervan, 2002.

———. *The Glory and the Shame*. Guildford, UK: Eagle, 1994.

———. "*The Significance and Potential of Pentecostalism*." In Hocken et al., *New Heaven? New Earth?* London: Darton, Longman & Todd, 1976; Springfield, IL: Templegate, 1977.

———. *The Strategy of the Spirit?* Guildford, UK: Eagle, 1996.

Hunter, Harold D., and Peter D. Hocken, eds. *All Together in One Place: Theological Papers from the Brighton Conference on World Evangelization*. Sheffield: Sheffield Academic Press, 1993.

International Catholic Charismatic Renewal Services Doctrinal Commission. *Baptism in the Holy Spirit*. Locust Grove, VA: National Service Committee, 2012.

Jaramillo, Diego. "It Can be Done: El Minuto de Dios." International Catholic Charismatic Renewal Office: *International Newsletter* 15, no. 4 (July–Aug 1989) 2.

Jenkins, Philip. *The Next Christendom: The Coming of Global Christianity*. Rev. ed. Oxford: Oxford University Press, 2007.

John Paul II. Meeting with Ecclesial Movements and New Communities, Pentecost, May 30, 1998. No Pages. Online: www.vatican.va/holy_father/john_paul_ii/speeches/1998/may/documents/hf_jp-ii_spe_19980530_riflessioni_en.html.

Kärkkäinen, Veli-Matti. *An Introduction to Ecclesiology.* Downers Grove, IL: InterVarsity, 2002.

Kasper, Walter. "Address to the College of Cardinals." The Pontifical Council for Promoting Christian Unity. *Information Service* 126 (2007) 185–88.

———. *A Handbook of Spiritual Ecumenism.* Hyde Park, NY: New City, 2006.

Kollins, Kim. *It's Only the Beginning.* Crowborough, UK: Highland, 1989.

Lamb, Charles B. *Path of Hope in Ireland.* Tipperary: CBL Services, 1983.

Macchia, Frank. *Baptized in the Spirit.* Grand Rapids, MI: Zondervan, 2006.

———. *Justified in the Spirit.* Grand Rapids, MI: Eerdmans, 2010.

MacNutt, Francis. "Latin America: Report from Fr. Francis MacNutt." *NC* (Nov 1971) 1–7.

Mansfield, Patti Gallagher. *As By a New Pentecost.* Rev. ed. Stonyhurst, UK: Proclaim!, 1992.

McDonnell, Kilian. *The Charismatic Renewal and Ecumenism.* New York: Paulist, 1978.

———, ed. *Open the Windows: The Popes and Charismatic Renewal.* South Bend, IN: Greenlawn, 1989.

Mills, Brian, and Roger Mitchell. *Sins of the Fathers: How National Repentance Removes Obstacles to Revival.* Tonbridge, UK: Sovereign World, 1999.

Newman, John Henry. *Lectures on the Present Position of Catholics in England.* London: Longmans, Green, 1908.

———. *On Consulting the Faithful in Matters of Doctrine.* Edited by John Coulson. London: Geoffrey Chapman, 1961.

O'Connor, Edward. *The Pentecostal Movement in the Catholic Church.* Notre Dame, IN: Ave Maria Press, 1971.

Omenyo, Cephas. *Pentecost Outside Pentecostalism: A Study of the Development of Charismatic Renewal in the Mainline Churches of Ghana.* Zoetermeer, NL: Boekencentrum, 2002.

Orellana, Luis, and Bernardo Campos, eds. *Ecumenismo del Espíritu: Pentecostalismo, Unidad y Misión.* Lima: Foro Pentecostal Latinoamericano, 2012.

Pontifical Council for Interreligious Dialogue et al. Christian Witness in a Multi-Religious World: Recommendations for Conduct. June 2011.

Quebedeaux, Richard. *The New Charismatics II.* San Francisco: Harper & Row, 1983.

Ranaghan, Kevin, and Dorothy Ranaghan. *Catholic Pentecostals.* Paramus, NJ: Paulist, 1969.

Roman Catholic-Pentecostal Dialogue. "Evangelization, Proselytism, and Common Witness." *Information Service* 97 (1998) 38–54.

Sherrill, John. *They Speak with Other Tongues.* Old Tappan, NJ: Fleming H. Revell, 1964.

Stilp, Deporres. "Tenth Anniversary of the Korean Catholic Charismatic Renewal January 1971–January 1981." *Korea Pastoral Xchange* 9, no. 1 (Jan–Feb 1981) 4–8.

Streeter, B. H. *The Primitive Church: Studied with Special Reference to the Origins of Christian Ministry.* London: Macmillan, 1929.

Suenens, Léon-Joseph. *Ecumenism and Charismatic Renewal: Theological and Pastoral Orientations, Malines Document 2.* Ann Arbor, MI: Servant Books, 1978.

———. *A New Pentecost?* Translated by Francis Martin. New York: Seabury, 1975.

Synan, Vinson. *Charismatic Bridges.* Ann Arbor, MI: Word of Life, 1974.

Theological and Pastoral Orientations on the Catholic Charismatic Renewal. Notre Dame, IN: Word of Life, 1974.

Toward Jerusalem Council II: Vision, Origin and Documents. Dallas, TX: TJCII, 2010.

Tugwell, Simon. *Did You Receive the Spirit?* London: Darton, Longman & Todd, 1971.

Bibliography

Vaccaro, Gabriel. *Aportes del Pentecostalismo al Movimiento Ecumenico*. Quito: CLAI, 1991.

Van Beek, Huibert, ed. *Revisioning Christian Unity: The Global Christian Forum*. Oxford: Regnum, 2009.

Viviers 1973: Rencontre Charismatique Interconfessionnelle. Valence-sur-Rhone: Réunies, 1974.

Weber, Jeremy. "Argentine Evangelicals Say Bergoglio as Pope Francis Is 'Answer To Our Prayers.'" *Christianity Today* (March 14, 2013). No Pages. Online: http://www.christianitytoday.com/ct/2013/march-web-only/argentine-evangelicals-say-bergoglio-as-pope-francis-is-ans.html.

Weigel, George. *Evangelical Catholicism: Deep Reform in the 21st-Century Church*. New York: Basic, 2013.

Wilkerson, David. *The Cross and the Switchblade*. New York: Bernard Geis, 1963.

Name Index

Subject Index

Printed in the USA
CPSIA information can be obtained
at www.ICGtesting.com
LVHW011051161023
761222LV00019B/338